Gender Identity, Sexuality and Autism

by the same author

Marriage and Lasting Relationships with Asperger's Syndrome (Autism Spectrum Disorder)
Successful Strategies for Couples or Counselors
Eva A. Mendes
ISBN 978 1 84905 999 2
eISBN 978 0 85700 981 4

of related interest

Trans Voices
Becoming Who You Are
Declan Henry
Foreword by Professor Stephen Whittle, OBE
Afterword by Jane Fae
ISBN 978 1 78592 240 4
eISBN 978 1 78450 520 2

Transitioning Together
One Couple's Journey of Gender and Identity Discovery
Wenn B. Lawson and Beatrice M. Lawson
ISBN 978 1 78592 103 2
eISBN 978 1 78450 365 9

The Autism Spectrum Guide to Sexuality and Relationships
Understand Yourself and Make Choices that are Right for You
Dr Emma Goodall
Forewords by Dr Wenn Lawson and Jeanette Purkis
ISBN 978 1 84905 705 9
eISBN 978 1 78450 226 3

An Aspie's Guide to Intimacy, Dating, Sex and Marriage
Been There. Done That. Try This!
Edited by Tony Attwood, Craig R. Evans and Anita Lesko
eISBN 978 1 78450 127 3

Love, Partnership, or Singleton on the Autism Spectrum
Edited by Luke Beardon, PhD and Dean Worton
ISBN 978 1 78592 206 0
eISBN 978 1 78450 484 7

The Partner's Guide to Asperger Syndrome
Susan Moreno, Marci Wheeler and Kealah Parkinson
ISBN 978 1 84905 878 0
eISBN 978 0 85700 566 3

Love, Sex and Long-Term Relationships
What People with Asperger Syndrome Really Really Want
Sarah Hendrickx
ISBN 978 1 84310 605 0
eISBN 978 1 84642 764 0

GENDER IDENTITY, SEXUALITY AND AUTISM

Voices from Across the Spectrum

EVA A. MENDES and MEREDITH R. MARONEY

Foreword by Wenn B. Lawson

Jessica Kingsley *Publishers*
London and Philadelphia

First published in 2019
by Jessica Kingsley Publishers
73 Collier Street
London N1 9BE, UK
and
400 Market Street, Suite 400
Philadelphia, PA 19106, USA

www.jkp.com

Copyright © Eva A. Mendes and Meredith R. Maroney 2019
Foreword copyright © Wenn B. Lawson 2019

Front cover image copyright © Chie Yasuda.

All rights reserved. No part of this publication may be reproduced in any material form (including photocopying, storing in any medium by electronic means or transmitting) without the written permission of the copyright owner except in accordance with the provisions of the law or under terms of a licence issued in the UK by the Copyright Licensing Agency Ltd. www.cla.co.uk or in overseas territories by the relevant reproduction rights organisation, for details see www.ifrro.org. Applications for the copyright owner's written permission to reproduce any part of this publication should be addressed to the publisher.

Warning: The doing of an unauthorised act in relation to a copyright work may result in both a civil claim for damages and criminal prosecution.

Library of Congress Cataloging in Publication Data
A CIP catalog record for this book is available from the Library of Congress

British Library Cataloguing in Publication Data
A CIP catalogue record for this book is available from the British Library

ISBN 978 1 78592 754 6
eISBN 978 1 78450 585 1

Printed and bound by CPI Group (UK) Ltd, Croydon, CR0 4YY

Dedicated to my mentor, Daisaku Ikeda
and his wife Kaneko Ikeda
And, my partner Deepanjan Das
With deepest appreciation and gratitude

Eva

Dedicated to the clients and
participants who have shared their
stories with me over the years

Meredith

Contents

Part 3: Discussion

Foreword

The stories you will read in this book are representative of a much higher percentage of the population than you might think. In one study, not only did the researchers find LGBTQ+ was twice as common in the autistic population than in the non-autistic population but it also found such differences were more common than heterosexuality (George and Stokes, 2018). We know that 40% of the trans community live with poor mental health and suicidality. This being so, how much more important is it that we take note and are ready to truly listen?

When I first visited the psychiatrist to talk about my own gender dysphoria/congruence, he didn't listen to me. He heard the word "autistic" and, instead of going beyond this, he stopped there. Instead of taking a few sessions with me to sort out my questions and explore the way forward, he took nearly a year of my already ageing life (I was 61 years old at that time) to conclude that which I already knew. There's something amiss about needing "Others" to be the authority over this aspect of our lives, to be the authority who gives us permission to be ourselves.

For some professionals, hearing the word "autistic" means they conclude certain things about a person. Initially they may wonder if an autistic person can "know" themselves well enough to be gender questioning. They may be aware that autism is a developmental disposition, and the delays due to autism may cause the professional to think an individual will "grow out" of their gender questioning state and, with time, settle down. The professional may ask themselves if the gender or sexuality considerations are due to an obsession or to sensory dysphoria. The point is, if you don't listen to our stories and journey with us, we may never know.

Who Am I

When looking out upon the world
I see as any might,
The things I notice, boy or girl
Are captured within my sight.
When looking out upon the world
I feel as any might
My heart can hurt, ache or break
My senses heightened, set or curled
I live through day and night.
But, as you look in upon my world
Your head might judge, your eyes not see,
The true reality that makes up me
Flesh and bone of body image
May not make the man
The clothes I wear, may cause a stare,
My choices may confuse.
But what if she is not I am?
What if he is not a man?
This binary world imposed
Is set by those who propose,
Male and female is set in time
When reality says there's not one line.

Moving away from seeing autism as a disorder and thinking of us as being "differently abled," due to our "diff-ability," is a huge, but natural, step forward. Autism awareness has been with us for some time now, but we need to move beyond awareness and into actioning our knowledge and understanding. Popular television shows like *The Good Doctor* and *The Muppet Show* have served to familiarize us with autism through their characters. This has helped to reduce fear and ignorance of autism, which is a good thing. Slowly, but surely, we are moving towards acceptance of autism as part of a naturally neurodiverse human population.

As stated in the Introduction to this book, "By conceptualizing autism as a cultural identity, rather than a disability, the discourse is changed to one of empowerment, rather than stigma or discrimination" (p.26).

So, the stage is set for the next chapter in autism history (herstory or their story). Understanding ourselves as "whole people" and having a deep sense of our own personhood is the connection needed to appreciate "I."

A dear friend and I were having a conversation today in which we discussed the concept of "I," the first letter in the word "Identity." I explained why it had taken me such a long time to "join the dots" with my own journey towards gender discovery and identity. For most of my life I had referred to myself as "Wendy," the name given to me by my parents at birth. For example, instead of saying, "I need to sit down," I would say, "Wendy needs to sit down." When I was asked, "Why do you refer to yourself in the third person?" I answered, "If you are 'I' and he is 'I,' who am 'I'? I'm Wendy."

As a child I rarely felt unhappy and was blissfully unaware of danger – an outgoing adventurous child, with an expectation life would be wonderful. I spent my later teenage years and young adult to mid-adult life, however, fighting anxiety, depression, disconnection. Over a period of 25 years I was in and out of mental health "hospitals," with no real understanding of why I felt so lost.

Finally, gaining my current diagnosis of autism at the age of 42, I thought all my inner dislocation and learning difficulties were because of my autism. It was uncomfortable realizing this, but it was also a relief. At last I had an answer! I put my total distancing of myself from puberty down to sensory overwhelm. I practiced standing to pee and wore tight clothing to flatten my breasts, believing this might stop me "growing up into an adult woman with all the associated discomforts." Later, I explained my sexual attraction to women as a dawning or awakening to being lesbian but never felt at home in that community.

Discovering my true center and becoming "I" took another 30 years. It was only four and a half years ago, at the age of 62, that I finally called myself "I" and let go of Wendy. I now live as Wenn, a trans guy, finally joined up and finally home.

I appreciate we are all different, as the stories in this book illustrate. Being autistic and living with a sexuality and/or a gender identity that does not fit neatly into the bell-shaped curve of "average" is confronting. For so many people it causes much anxiety, confusion and pain. However, I believe there has never been a better time for those of us living as autistic individuals who happen to be LGBTQ+

to find our tribe. With the arrival of the Internet and so many ways to discover "connection," we need never be out in the cold again.

It's our time! Being autistic will mean being single-focused and easily taken up with those things that interest us. We often operate within the narrow beam of the torch light, intensely attending to those things seen within it. In the non-autistic world, people have access to the wider torch beam so their attention tends to be spread more broadly—often not so intensely—and they are able to notice the bigger picture. This is harder for us. Not noticing the bigger picture has benefits for some. In some stories you will read in this book individuals always knew their true gender and/or sexuality. They only saw the "I" of who they were, despite the picture given to them by others. For others though, operating with single focus caused confusion and fear. They only saw the picture given by others and didn't connect to their true "I" for many years. However we get there, by whatever means and for how ever long it takes, arriving at our final destination and finding ourselves home at last, is a joy that is beyond expression.

As you read this book, you may find your story represented and identify with the experiences of others. This might be encouraging for you and act to further cement your knowledge and journey to date. For others, this book may be a challenge to read and may cause you some discomfort. If this happens to you, please continue with us and don't give in to the disquiet within you. Some places we visit are uncomfortable to start with—after all, we haven't been there before.

I was once at an autism conference and heard a speaker say: "autistic individuals are asexual and don't connect to their sexuality." I was horrified! Some individuals are asexual, not because they don't connect to being a sexual being but because they are not interested in being sexually active with another human being. According to the Asexual Visibility and Education Network (AVEN, 2018):

> Unlike celibacy, which is giving up sex as a choice, being asexual is an orientation, like being gay or straight. Asexual people still crave connections with people and often form romantic relationships with others—they have the same emotional needs as any other person; they just don't necessarily exchange bodily fluids.

But, this is still the exception rather than the rule. Being autistic doesn't knock out your sexuality; it just means it might take longer to join the dots (in that journey of self-discovery) due to being singly focused. As you will read in this book, connecting to one's sexuality and gender happens differently for different people. The autistic lens is an added factor which sometimes simplifies things because an individual might not be so concerned with social norms or with what others may think. On the other hand, it may complicate things as an individual struggles to put all the pieces of the gender/sexuality puzzle into their right place.

Intersectionality isn't uncommon and, as humans, we are all made up of various parts: race, ethnicity, spirituality, disability, the various "caps" we wear and so on. Somehow though, when it comes to sexuality and gender, people are expected to fit into rigid boxes. Of course, traditional models of patriarchy and matriarchy carry some responsibility for this. Politics and religion are also implicated in the long story of what's expected of human behavior. Yet, the story changes over time and according to circumstances. For example, women were "allowed" to do the work instead of men when men were not available during World War II. This ability to be flexible in times of need is seen very much as a neurologically typical prerogative. In autism though, we have always been simply "who we are." As the stories in this book illustrate, the need to be honest, truthful and open, and to live with integrity, governs the autistic population. Our ability to live and to love the person we relate to, whatever their gender, is often uppermost. We are said to be rigid in our disposition, yet, apart from being true to ourselves and our passions, we are often much less rigid when it comes to gender fluidity and sexuality than the typical population.

I trust you will read this book with an open mind and find within its pages an echo of true humanity. As autistic people we may take time to connect with all that the "I" in our identity means. Sometimes we need support, as do all humans, to discover how the parts all go together. The art of interoception and connectivity to this eighth sense, can be off-line in autism. Most non-autistic individuals connect more easily to the inner knowledge of knowing and of being who they are. Awareness of hunger or fullness, of breathing and heart rate, of being cold or hot, of pain or comfort, of muscles being tight or relaxed, of being male, female, or both, of having sexual desire or not, is not always a given. Sound interoception can take time and effort to build. When those around us listen to our stories with understanding and not judgement, walk with us through the tasks of self-discovery, and respond to the needs that emerge, we have a better chance of getting things right. Fear is a negative response to the unknown. Rather than responding with fear of what you don't know, get to know our stories, get to know us.

Wenn B. Lawson (PhD)

www.wennlawson.com

Acknowledgments

Eva

This book would not be possible without the contributions of the 19 participants who so generously committed their stories to this book, so that we may help and encourage those countless others around the world in similar situations. An honorable mention also to all the numerous clients and their partners and spouses that I've had the fortune to work with through the years, who continue to inspire me to do better each day.

I'm grateful to my publisher, JKP, and Dania Jekel, my mentor and former supervisor at AANE (Asperger/Autism Network), who influenced some of the initial thoughts and ideas that kickstarted the book.

My deepest appreciation for Nisha Narvekar, friend and colleague, for the long discussions on various topics, and for offering suggestions, sage advice, and assistance in the editing of the book. I would like to express my gratitude to all my Buddhist friends in the Soka Gakkai International for their constant care and encouragement. A special thanks to my partner, Deepanjan Das, and our families for their unwavering love and support.

Above all, I would like to thank my co-author, Meredith, also without whom this book would not be possible. Thank you. So grateful for your guidance, expertise, and willingness to go on this journey with me.

Meredith

Thank you to my family, friends, and partner for your ongoing support.

I greatly appreciate all that I've learned from mentors and supervisors, particularly at Aspire and UMass Boston, as I've grown as a clinician and researcher.

Thank you to Eva for your continued support and knowledge through the process.

I feel privileged to be doing this work and am grateful to everyone who was willing to share their stories in this book.

Part 1

INTRODUCTION

GENDER IDENTITY, SEXUALITY AND AUTISM

Voices from Across the Spectrum

An East Indian client of mine—Eva's—whom we shall call Nitin,[1] 18, came to the United States to start school as an undergrad at a well-known engineering school in Boston. He entered counseling at the behest of his parents due to depression in his second semester. In addition to addressing his depression, Nitin also had many questions around what he saw as his autism spectrum difference (ASD) traits (Table 1 in the next chapter, Terminology Tables, explains the terminology used throughout this book). He did very well academically, as evidenced by his enrollment into the prestigious engineering school, but by the second semester he reported:

> I'm feeling really lonely and depressed. I have trouble making friends easily and I also think I might be gay. And, my dad has been really hard on me lately. He keeps telling me how I have to do really well in school because he's spending so much money for my education. Also, I think I might have undiagnosed Asperger's because I'm very much like those characters in the TV show *Big Bang Theory*, but I just manage to hide it really well. I haven't made any friends here at all. I'm in my room a lot. And the academics are tough and I'm not that good at organizing and time management. When I'm feeling down, I tend to play video games a lot and lose track of time and often get behind on schoolwork. Because I'm smart, I can usually cram and get through, but I feel really stressed out and down most of the time.

1 Name and identifying details changed to protect client confidentiality.

As the session progressed, Nitin continued:

> My dad would hate it if he knew that I was gay. I think my mom already knows, but we've never talked about it openly. A friend of mine in India knows about it, but she's a lesbian, so she guessed that I was too...urh...gay too I mean. I would really, really like a boyfriend, but I've never even kissed a guy before, and I can't even make friends, so having a boyfriend seems like a far-fetched dream. Lately, my anxiety is getting bad as well. I've been hating the way my body is too. I wish I were better-looking. I bet like most people wouldn't even find me attractive.

Cases like Nitin's are rather common in the ASD community. In my—Eva's—practice as psychotherapist and counselor, there have been an increasing number of individuals on the autism spectrum, similar to Nitin, who identify as being on the spectrums of autism, gender identity, and sexual orientation.

Gender and Sexual Orientation Diversity—Prevalence within ASD Individuals

Since Asperger Syndrome first emerged as an official diagnosis in the *Diagnostic and Statistical Manual of Mental Disorders DSM-IV* (American Psychiatric Association, 2000), our knowledge and understanding of adults on the autism spectrum has increased and deepened, and now we are in an era of emerging evidence that suggests that autistic individuals are more likely to identify as lesbian, gay, bisexual, transgender, queer/questioning, intersex, and asexual (LGBTQ) than non-autistic individuals. Prevalence rates of autism spectrum difference are estimated to be one in 59 or 1.69% (Baio *et al.*, 2018), while it is estimated that almost 4.1% adults identity as LGBTQ (Gates, 2017). There are a number of studies that have highlighted the increasing diversity of sexual orientation and gender identity, although there is still very little discussion on the overlap of being autistic and LGBTQ, particularly from the perspective of those who hold these identities. Even much of the research on autism has excluded the perspectives and experiences of autistic individuals themselves. Furthermore, such research has tended to be largely diagnostic, using labels like autism spectrum disorder and gender dysphoria (formerly known as Gender

Identity Disorder), which can be pathologizing, and may not fit with the way individuals view their own experiences, although such studies have increased awareness for those living at the intersection.

Our book aims to present a diverse range of voices from ASD-LGBTQ individuals, as well as some brief reflections from their partners and parents, and clinical perspectives from Eva, a psychotherapist and autism specialist, and Meredith, a researcher and clinician also working and researching at this intersection.

A number of studies have highlighted the diversity of sexual orientation or gender identity in ASD individuals. For instance, a review of recent studies on this topic found that children diagnosed with autism spectrum difference were approximately 7.59% more likely to present with gender variance than non-autistic individuals (Strang *et al.*, 2016). Another study found that approximately 7.8% of children who were diagnosed with gender dysphoria (GD), could meet the criteria for a diagnosis of ASD (de Vries *et al.*, 2010). In an online survey of autistic women, it was found that 50% of autistic individuals versus 21% of non-autistic individuals (within a total sample of 248 people) reported their gender identity as either trans, non-binary, or genderqueer (Bush, 2016). Finally, in a study of gender identity and sexual orientation of individuals with ASD, significantly higher rates of gender dysphoria were present among autistic individuals than in the general population (George and Stokes, 2017).

Several recent studies with autistic individuals have noted greater diversity of sexual orientation among autistic individuals (Barnett and Maticka-Tyndale, 2015; Hellemans *et al.*, 2007). In a qualitative study with adults on the autism spectrum, 17% identified as bisexual or queer and 13% identified as lesbian or gay when reporting sexual orientation (Barnett and Maticka-Tyndale, 2015). Another study, comprised of a sample of 208 ASD participants, found that approximately 84% reported their sexual orientation as non-heterosexual (Bush, 2016). More recent research found that autistic individuals, particularly autistic women, reported feelings of sexual attraction to same-sex partners to a greater degree than the general population (DeWinter, De Graaf, and Begeer, 2017). This exploration of autism traits and diversity of sexual orientation was recently conducted in Stockholm, with authors finding that those who met the criteria for autism (as defined by the Autism Spectrum Quotient, also known as AQ-10) were more likely to identify their sexual orientation as bisexual, or incapable of fitting within the labels of either heterosexual, homosexual, or bisexual (Rudolph *et al.*, 2017).

Critiques on Overlapping Identities

There have been some critiques on the idea that there is an increased likelihood to be diverse in gender and sexual orientation among autistic individuals. For instance, Turban and van Schalkwyk (2018) discuss the limitations with the present research in the ways that traits of gender diversity and autism are measured, calling into question whether or not there is a link between transgender identities and autism. Whether or not there is increased prevalence of diversity of sexual orientation and gender identity within individuals on the spectrum, the intersection of these LGBTQ and autistic identities has been widely discussed in online groups, platforms, and videos.

How This Book Came to Be

Eva's Work

Eva first became aware of these intersecting identities through her clinical work with ASD adults starting in 2009. Her very first client, during her undergraduate clinical counseling internship at the Asperger/Autism Network (AANE; formerly known as the Asperger's Association of New England), was an elderly woman who identified as bisexual and gender non-conforming and dressed in neutral androgynous clothing every day of her life, even on formal occasions. Even though she was celibate for most of her life, she had discovered her bisexuality and gender identity much before she had stumbled upon her autism diagnosis in her mid-50s. Shortly after, in her training as a couple's counselor, Eva started working with lesbian couples where one partner identified as being on the autism spectrum. Then, a couple of years ago, Eva was requested to facilitate a Gender Identity Support Group at AANE and did so for a period of one year. That's when she realized that gender was even more complex and diverse than she had ever considered. Since the very beginning of her career, Eva has primarily worked with the ASD adults and in particular couples where one partner identifies as being on the autism spectrum. The more time she spent with her clients, both in individual and group counseling settings, the more she began to gain exposure to an increasing number of clients who were non-conforming in their gender and sexual orientation.

In therapy, rather than challenging their narratives and experiences, Eva listened by suspending judgment and keeping an open mind. In doing so, she realized that there were misconceptions and fallacies that continued to be held by those in certain medical-neuropsychological-mental health circles: 1) the belief that autism only affects those visibly impaired; and 2) the idea that individuals with autism, even adults, were unable to adequately understand their sexual orientation and gender identity.

The misjudgements and questions in the medical community mean that many autistic individuals have to deal with, and often suffer through, the gate-keeping and barriers posed by medical doctors in keeping these individuals from opting for gender-affirming surgeries.

In the neuropsychological field, it means that these individuals are being routinely misdiagnosed or that they don't fit the diagnosis to the last letter in the *DSM*. Many counselors who are uninformed about ASD say to their clients, "You're not stuck staring at cracks in the sidewalk, or rocking in a dark corner, or sitting in the basement of your mother's couch playing video games all day, so you definitely don't have Asperger's/autism and it would be a waste of time to even pursue a diagnosis."

Many clinicians also also try to "convince" their clients that they will "outgrow" their asexuality or genderqueerness as ASD is a developmental disorder and in time, they will be able to feel better in their assigned bodies. Therefore, after writing her first book, *Marriage and Lasting Relationships with Asperger's Syndrome* (2015), which included some same-sex relationship narratives, Eva realized that she needed to further explore her study of the overlap of autism, gender identity, and sexual orientation to put out information for autistic individuals, their families, partners, and clinicians.

Meredith's Work

Meredith first became interested in these intersecting identities through her clinical work with young adults and adolescents on the autism spectrum. As she worked with autistic individuals, particularly around the issues of relationships and dating, it became clear that many of the interventions were heteronormative in nature, and often failed to acknowledge the sexual orientation and gender identity of these individuals, with an emphasis on socially scripted behaviors. She observed misconceptions in the literature and clinical worlds, which tended to overlook autistic individuals as sexual beings who engaged in relationships and were capable of identifying their sexual orientation and gender identity. She continued this line of research while beginning her PhD, bringing together her interests in LGBTQ issues and autistic individuals through a qualitative exploration of the experiences of trans autistic individuals. She is currently working on her dissertation, which focuses on an expressive writing intervention for autistic LGBTQ individuals.

Meredith and Eva connected through a conference on the clinical implications for working with gender diverse and autistic individuals, and have brought together their respective experiences with research and clinical work to connect to individuals who were interested in sharing their experiences in this particular format.

Who You'll Hear from in the Book

Diversity in Terms of Age and Race

Individuals in this book come from a variety of backgrounds, with diversity in age, race, and social class. Ages range from 21 to 50, with the average age being approximately 31 years old. All individuals have attended at least one college, with the majority reporting they have obtained or are working on a bachelor's degree, and one who has received her master's degree. They are working in a variety of fields, including engineering, law, illustration, creative writing, and occupations such as a cook and semi-retired arborist.

The majority of participants have been seen by Eva in either group or individual therapy. The remainder of the autistic participants were recruited through professional and personal connections, while one was found online. The family and partner perspectives were recruited from autistic participants in this book. For example, you'll hear from Maya and Violet, who are partners, as well as Xiomara and her mother, Myra. Despite strong efforts to gain greater representation of black or African American identified participants through online recruitment and reaching out to organizations, we were only able to find one participant who was interested in participating in this project. This is interesting to consider given the biases found in autism diagnosis. For instance, women are less likely to be diagnosed with autism (Kreiser and White, 2014), and some research has found disparities in the diagnosis of autism among racial and ethnic minorities (Mandell *et al.*, 2009).

Differences in Diagnoses

Although the majority of our participants have had access to high-quality clinical support, due to living in an area with access to knowledgeable providers, many still had a lot of difficulty finding clinicians who truly understood their diagnosis and experience. Our participants were diagnosed at all ages. Some were diagnosed as children or adolescents and some pursued a formal diagnosis in adulthood through a psychotherapist or a neuropsychologist; one individual received a formal evaluation, but her evaluators were not experts and therefore could not confirm this diagnosis, which is a common experience of people who pursue an ASD diagnosis in adulthood. A couple of our participants were self-identified/diagnosed, which has become increasingly common for ASD individuals (Lehnhardt *et al.*, 2013). You will notice variability in the ways participants label their autism, such as: Asperger Syndrome, Autism Spectrum Disorder (ASD), official ASD diagnosis, self-diagnosed autism, Nonverbal Learning Disability (NVLD).

Other most common co-occurring diagnoses were depression, anxiety, and Attention Deficit Hyperactivity Disorder (ADD/ADHD).

The differences in diagnoses reflects both changes in the *Diagnostic and Statistical Manual of Mental Disorders* (*DSM-5*; American Psychiatric Association, 2013), as well as how the person sought out the diagnosis. For instance, some participants received an Asperger Syndrome diagnosis, which is no longer in the *DSM-5*, although many people choose to continue identifying in this way (Giles, 2014). Some individuals may choose to seek out a clinical assessment in order to receive documentation for the "official" diagnosis, which can provide access to services.

Variations in Identities in Gender and Sexual Orientation

Participants labeled their gender identities with the following terms: cisgender female, cisgender male, gender non-conforming, agender, non-binary, binary trans man, both male and female, and Tankgirl. There were differences in the ways our participants chose or had the opportunity to affirm their gender identities. For instance, you will hear from Alyia, who chose to medically transition, as well as others like Cliff, who does want to have top surgery, but hasn't yet due to difficulties with accessing services and lack of family support. Others still did not feel that gender confirmation surgery was necessary for them.

Our participants also qualified their sexual orientation in diverse ways. The terms bisexual, pansexual, lesbian, queer, asexual, panromantic, various, gay, and I like everyone were all used to state their preferred orientation.

Relationships

Some of our participants reported being single, while some were partnered, married, and in polyamorous relationships.

Through reading our participants' stories, you will discover the diversity of experiences of being autistic, as well as being gender non-conforming and the varieties of sexual orientation.

Voices from Across the Spectrum

A critical study reported that the perspectives of autistic adults are often missing from the literature on autism and that autistic individuals often held more knowledge than their family members and providers and described autism more experientially, illustrating the importance of considering autistic adults the experts in research (Gillespie-Lynch *et al.*, 2017). Others have reflected on the importance of understanding autism through the lived experiences of autistic individuals (Jones *et al.*, 2014; Jones *et al.*, 2012), but few have explored this from a lens of diversity of sexual orientation and/or gender identity. In a qualitative study focused on the experiences of transgender autistic individuals, participants expressed appreciation about having a space to discuss their intersecting identities, and reported being excited to share study findings with others in their life, such as their providers (Maroney and Horne, 2018). Although individuals who are ASD-LGBTQ are gaining more attention in research and certain clinical circles, there is a lot to learn about their identities and experiences, and how to best support them clinically.

In this book, we've provided a space for queer and autistic people to share their experiences, within the framework that autistic LGBTQ individuals are presenting with diverse intersectioning neurological, sexual orientation, and gender identities. Neurodiversity conceptualizes autistic identity as neurological differences rather than impairments; the distinction is that differences in socialization and communication do not require a cure, but, rather, deserve equal respect to those who are deemed to be neurotypical (Ortega, 2009). By conceptualizing autism as a cultural identity, rather than a disability, the discourse is changed to one of empowerment, rather than stigma or discrimination (Parsloe, 2015), making it essential that these voices are prioritized in conversations on gender identity and sexual orientation with ASD adults. Our book attempts to fill a void in the existing literature by bringing together the voices of adults who identify as ASD and LGBTQ, their parents and partners, as well as clinical reflections by us—Meredith and Eva. In order to provide the broadest perspective and widest lens possible, we've done our best to include autistic individuals from a wide variety of backgrounds, ages, races, ethnicities, identities and orientations.

Who This Book Is For

This book is particularly recommended if you're someone on the autism spectrum and also have divergent gender and sexual orientation identities. We hope that these narratives will help you validate your own experiences and help you to better navigate your journey of discovery, affirmation, and diagnosis.

We hope that these perspectives and narratives will once and for all shift the perception in some medical and mental health circles that individuals on the autism spectrum may be unable or incapable of knowing who they are as it relates to their gender identities, sexual orientation, and even neuropsychology. In addition to autistic and LGBTQ individuals, we've interviewed parents and romantic partners of our participants. By providing first-person accounts of what it is like to live with ASD and divergent gender identities and sexual orientations in a non-ASD, cishet (see page 32) world, our aim is to create awareness and allies amongst those who can have the biggest impact in the lives of these individuals, particularly parents, partners, caregivers, educators, employers, and clinicians. We invite you all to read on and discover a group of remarkable, resilient, courageous people who identify as being on these various spectrums.

Of course, we would also like for the general public to read this book so that they can form a broader perspective and a better understanding of the overlapping identities of ASD-LGBTQ. We hope that as our knowledge and appreciation of the ASD-LGBTQ overlap continues to widely spread, we will be able to uproot misconceptions and eliminate the too oft seen tragedies of hatred and violence. Our goal is for the voices and stories in our book to help in creating a lasting culture of peace and acceptance in a world that welcomes and nurtures people of all neurological makeups, genders, and sexual orientations. Additionally, we hope that our book further encourages clinicians, family members, educators, and employers in their compassionate support and accommodations of ASD-LGBTQ adults.

TERMINOLOGY TABLES

Table 1: Autism/Asperger Syndrome

What is Autism/Asperger Syndrome? "Autism is a neurological condition that fundamentally affects how a person experiences the world" (Bumiller, 2008, p.974), which may include differences in the way environment, sensory information, or social knowledge is processed. There are a number of terms, both diagnostic and more informal, to describe the experience of being on the autism spectrum. Several commonly used terms are listed below.	
Asperger Syndrome (AS)	The diagnosis of Asperger Syndrome was removed from the *Diagnostic and Statistical Manual-5* (*DSM-5*) when it was released in 2013. Those who would have received an AS diagnosis in the past now receive a diagnosis of Autism Spectrum Disorder, Level 1, 2, or 3, based on their level of functioning. However, AS is still widely used colloquially by clinicians and those on the spectrum themselves and their families.
Aspie	An affectionate term for a person with Asperger Syndrome. It is often used by Aspies.
Autistic	This is often used as an identity for people in the Autism Community, who identify with the traits associated with Autism Spectrum Disorder, and may or may not have received a diagnosis. Autistic identity stems from an identity-first understanding, rather than person-first. This is often debated across groups (i.e. Autism Community vs. Parents or Providers).
Autism Spectrum Difference (ASD)	In this book we have used the acronym ASD to indicate Autism Spectrum Difference, because we feel that the word "disorder" is disempowering and discriminatory, whereas the term "difference" implies that ASD is simply a different neurological mindset—different, but not disordered or less than. In addition to representing people with ASD, this book may be useful to people and their families and partners diagnosed with Social (pragmatic) Communication Disorder (SCD), Non-Verbal Learning Disorder (NVLD), High-Functioning Autism (HFA), Pervasive Developmental Disorder-Not Otherwise Specified, Childhood Disintegrative Disorder, Autistic Disorder and Attention Deficit Hyperactivity Disorder (ADHD).

Non-Spectrum (NS)/Non-ASD/Non-Autistic	The term "non-spectrum" refers to people that don't have ASD. In the past, non-spectrum (NS) individuals have been known as neurotypical (NT). However, even if a person isn't autistic, they often have neurological differences other than ASD. These can include Attention Deficit Hyperactivity Disorder (ADHD), dyslexia, learning differences, bipolar disorder, seizure disorders, etc. Therefore, we prefer to refer to non-autistic people as non-NS (Mendes, 2015), non-ASD, or non-autistic.
Neurodiversity	Similar to biodiversity, neurodiversity refers to the naturally occurring variations and evolutionary adaptations of the human brain (Armstrong, 2010).
Neurodivergent	This is the opposite of neurotypical. It was made popular by the neurodiversity movement and refers to atypical neurological development and states. It includes autism and AS as well as dyslexia, Attention Deficit Hyperactivity Disorder (ADHD), Obsessive Compulsive Disorder (OCD), learning differences, and others.*

*See www.disabled-world.com for more information.

Table 2: Gender Identity

What is gender identity? Gender identity is one's internal, deeply held sense of one's gender. In our society, people are primed to have a gender identity either as a woman (if they are biologically female) or as male (if they are biologically male). For some individuals, their gender identity may not align with their biological sex. Also, some people notice changes in their gender identity over time. Regardless of their biological sex, people may identify as masculine, feminine, both, neither, or as other gender identities.	
Some commonly used gender identities	
Agender	Having no gender; not identifying as masculine, feminine, or another gender.
Bigender	Having two gender identities, which may be masculine, feminine, and/or other genders. The extent to which someone identifies as their two genders may or may not change over time, and it may or may not be influenced by context or environment.
Cisgender	"Cis" is a Latin prefix meaning "on the same side as," and is used to describe people whose gender identity is aligned with their sex assigned at birth (e.g. a female who identifies as a woman, a male who identifies as a man).

Demigirl	Identifying partially, but not completely as a woman, girl, or feminine. People who identify as demigirl may or may not have other gender identities too.
Genderfluid	Moving across genders or having a fluctuating gender identity. Changes may occur quickly or slowly, and these may or may not be influenced by context or environment.
Gender Non-Conforming/ Genderqueer/ Non-Binary	Not identifying exclusively as masculine or feminine, or as a cisgender man or woman, and not ascribing to the traditional gender roles and societal expectations of the gender associated with one's sex assigned at birth. These terms are often used interchangeably, although some people may prefer one over the other. Individuals with these identities may have either fixed or more fluid gender identities.
Pangender	Experiencing all genders; not identifying exclusively as masculine and/or feminine. Some pangender people experience genders that they cannot describe, or that society does not recognize.
Transgender	Having a gender identity that does not match the sex one was assigned at birth (i.e. a person assigned male at birth with a feminine gender identity, a person assigned female at birth with a masculine gender identity).
Other terms related to gender identity	
Gender Expression	This is also described as "gender presentation." The way someone chooses to express or display their gender through dress, social behavior, accessories, and mannerisms can vary in masculine and feminine traits or scales (Safe Zone Project, 2018).
Gender Pronouns	The pronouns people use to refer to themselves can include an endless variety of possible combinations. For instance, people may use he/him/his, she/her/her, or they/them/theirs, but they may also use he/they, or less commonly known ones such as ze or hir.*

*For more information see this helpful reference: www.mypronouns.org.

Note: The definitions presented in this table are adapted from those provided by the Safe Zone Project (2018), the GLAAD Media Reference Guide (2016), and recent scientific research on gender identity.

Source: Mendes and Bush, 2016

Table 3: Sexual Orientation

What is sexual orientation? An aspect of identity that captures the gender(s) of the individuals one feels sexually attracted to and/or engages in sexual activity with, in relation to one's own gender identity. Some people experience little or no variation in their sexual orientation or in the individuals they are attracted to, while others notice changes in their sexual orientation over time. Sexual orientation is related to, but ultimately different from, gender identity, as it refers to romantic/emotional/sexual/spiritual attraction.	
Commonly used terms to describe sexual orientation	
Asexual/Gray Asexual/ Graysexual/ Ace-Sexual	Not experiencing sexual attraction or desire towards others. "Aromantic" is often used to describe people who do not experience romantic and/or emotional attraction towards other people. People can be both asexual and aromantic, or they can be asexual but not aromantic, or aromantic but not asexual. People who identify as asexual may differ in their desire for solo sexual activity. People who identify as "gray asexual" may experience physical, romantic, and/or emotional attraction towards others, but in fewer contexts, with fewer people, and/or with less intensity relative to other people.
Bisexual	Experiencing sexual attraction towards individuals of two genders (usually men and women, but may include other genders).
Gay	Experiencing sexual attraction primarily towards individuals of one's own sex and/or gender (e.g. a woman who feels attraction toward other women). Some gay women prefer the term "lesbian," and others do not.
Heterosexual	Experiencing sexual attraction primarily towards individuals of the "opposite" sex (i.e. men who are attracted to women, and women who are attracted to men). Among people without ASD, this is the most common sexual orientation. Often referred to as "straight."
Pansexual	Experiencing sexual attraction towards individuals of any sex or gender, or of no gender; not limited in sexual attraction or choice towards any sex or gender.
Queer	Many choose to use this as an umbrella term for people who do not identify as straight. While queer is traditionally a pejorative term (i.e. a put-down), it has been appropriated/reclaimed by some gender and sexual minorities to describe themselves and their experiences. For some, the word "queer" has political connotations. Not everyone who identifies as a sexual minority also identifies as queer.

Note: The definitions presented in this table are adapted from those provided by the Safe Zone Project (2018), the GLAAD Media Reference Guide (2016), and recent scientific research on sexual orientation.

Source: Mendes and Bush, 2016

Other Key LGBTQ Terms

LGBTQ: For the sake of clarity, consistency with current literature, and readability, please know that we've used the abbreviated acronym of LGBTQ. This encompasses lesbian, gay, bisexual, transgender, queer/questioning, intersex, and asexual identities (LGBTQIA+), as well as ones that are not included in the acronym. It is considered to encompass a number of sexual orientation and gender identities.

Intersex: Someone whose combination of chromosomes, gonads, hormones, internal sex organs, and genitals differs from the two expected patterns of male or female (Safe Zone Project, 2018).

Cishet: Refers to someone who is both cisgender and heterosexual or straight.[1]

---

1 See www.queerdictionary.blogspot.com for more information.

DIVERSE NARRATIVES

Narratives illustrating the diversity of sexual orientation and gender identity as well as diversity in intersecting racial, ethnic and religious identities of autistic individuals living at these intersectionalities were intentionally prioritized. As stated by Shore (Mendes, 2015), "If you've met one person with autism, you've met one person with autism" (p,230). Therefore, it is essential that we keep in mind that no two autistic individuals' experiences are the same even though there might be some global themes and similarities in their stories. Included in the narratives are also affirmative perspectives from parents and partners.

Recruitment

Individuals were invited to participate in this book through prior connections, reaching out online, and through word-of-mouth. Those who chose to participate in this project reported wanting their stories to be able to help others.

How Interviews Were Conducted

Participants had the option to complete a written questionnaire or to sit with one of the authors for an individual interview, which was then transcribed. Most people opted to complete the written questionnaire independently, which gave them time to complete it at their leisure and in a preferred format. Interviews were edited for clarity, brevity, and cohesiveness. In editing these interviews, we found it important to alter the stories and experiences of those represented as little as possible, with the goal of making an accessible resource for individuals with ASD-LGBTQ identities, providers, partners, family members, and anyone interested in learning more.

Anonymity

In order to ensure anonymity, the real names of all participants in this book have been changed to pseudonyms. Additionally, identifying information such as where they work and live, and the names of associated people that the participants are talking about has also been modified. In order to best serve the people whose stories you will find in this book, protecting their privacy was discussed and deliberated on at length. Ultimately we decided to anonymize the narratives, as the majority of those who shared their stories were not out to everyone in their life with either their sexual orientation, gender identity, or autistic identity.

Compensation

Each person who participated was asked to review an informed consent form, and participants were free to ask questions about the project prior to their involvement. To compensate for the time and effort participants made while sharing their stories they were presented with gift cards and a copy of the finished book.

Part 2

THE NARRATIVES

Chapter 1

MAYA

I remember specifically having a sinking feeling and thinking "What if I'm a lesbian?"

I just couldn't imagine my life getting more complicated.

Name: Maya

Pronouns: She/Her

Age: 23

Education and Profession: Graduate student in Speech-Language Pathology

Living Situation: I live with my (female) partner of three years.

Diagnosis: I have an official diagnosis of Asperger's/autism. I was diagnosed as an adult.

Gender Identity: I am a cisgender woman.

Sexual Orientation(s): I consider myself queer. I mostly am interested in women, and am politically committed to surrounding myself with women, but I sometimes find myself interested in or thinking about men.

Being Diagnosed: My social and emotional issues appeared in first grade. However, I never received formal accommodations or special education in elementary or middle school. Informally, my classroom teachers would call my mother and consult with her for solutions to my school behavior (e.g. defiance, bossiness, not working well with other children, and meltdowns). This resulted in different types of informal accommodations throughout the years, such as "behavior charts" created for me and break cards (that I could give a teacher or that the teacher could give me). I was put in groups based on who I might work with best. I had no diagnostic label, so some teachers dismissed my behavior as spoiled, bratty, and noncompliant.

When I was 13, I began being taken to child psychologists. I was deeply depressed and anxious, and this had escalated to the point of being unable to tolerate most of my current (already restricted) diet. It was mistakenly suggested that my mother was simply in denial about my being anorexic. I definitely had avoidant/restrictive food intake disorder, and my sensory issues related to food were exacerbated by my heightened anxiety.

While I had some bad experiences with a psychotherapist who didn't understand me, a therapist seeing my brother (who was diagnosed autistic at age three) mentioned to my mother that she saw autistic traits in me.

I finally received a formal ASD diagnosis about a year ago.

I find that people are becoming more and more informed about ASD. Over the last two or three years there has been a bigger shift in understanding autistic self-advocacy, and the view of what autism is has widened. I think people are generally surprised when I say I'm autistic. Part of it is that I appear very functional, and part, I think, is just that I am an autistic woman, which people are sometimes caught off guard by. People all seem to have at least a surface understanding of ASD, since it became much more of a hot topic, and because there are so many people who are related to or know someone with autism, or someone who has an autistic child.

Medications: I began taking medication for depression/anxiety around age 13, and had several bad experiences with medications. Then I found one that was effective. The psychiatrist I met when I was around 15 was the only one I ever thought respected me, and I continued to see her throughout high school and on breaks while in college. Once I began taking medication, my relationship with my mother was able to progress because I spent less time being angry and sad.

I've been seeing my current psychiatrist now for a year. I believe she is helping me with the emotional awareness I've always struggled with, my meltdowns that stem from pushing myself too hard, and my relationship with my partner. She also is dynamic in adjusting the multiple psychiatric medications I am now on, so that I have maintained relative stability throughout graduate school.

My Mother and Father: My parents are both immigrants from Argentina. I have a younger brother who is autistic, and was diagnosed at age three. We are all culturally Jewish. My father has not been diagnosed but is almost certainly on the spectrum. He is a typical Silicon Valley techie.

Growing up, I had a complicated relationship with my mother. The difficulties I was having at school were reflected at home as well: everything set me off, I had breakdowns, I would say no and cry and generally struggled with self-regulation, and it showed. I would slam doors in my mother's face, become aggressive and/or self-injurious, and she struggled to understand me.

Our relationship improved once I left for college. We have been very close since then, and I think not living at home has been a large part of that. I tend to revert to old patterns when I go back home.

I am currently very close to my mother and she is a strong source of support. Although, in the past year, due to her marital problems and her separation from my father, she has had a difficult time herself, which has changed the dynamic of our relationship slightly. I am often offering her support these days, about her relationships, about how to help my brother, and about other stressors in her life.

Right now, I am closer to my father than I ever have been. He and I didn't really have any sort of relationship growing up. We existed in the same house, orbiting each other and sometimes crossing. He had a very low tolerance for my outbursts and stubbornness. He is inflexible in many ways, and so am I, so we clashed on many occasions. He tended to be reclusive, and was not very engaged in my childhood.

This year, my parents separated. It was very amicable. Since the separation, my relationship with my father has changed. Suddenly, he is calling me on the phone, just to talk. When I went home to visit, he would initiate asking to go out to lunch, or just suggesting spending more time together. I feel that having lost the connection to me through my mother, he is realizing that he has to work a little harder to stay updated on my life and to be present in it. I feel closer to him than before, and I feel that he is motivated to be in my life. He is learning more about himself through therapy, and has now begun to think about the way that being autistic has impacted his life.

Having a Sibling with Autism: My brother was classically autistic, and diagnosed at age three. He progressed quickly, and was fully mainstreamed by the end of elementary school. I went through a period where I hated my brother deeply. I still can't find the source of this, but my feeling is that it is related to his diagnosis and the focus on him for many years of my life. I would treat him horribly, and he looked up to me, always. I would blame my hatred on anything—his hair, his intrusion in my room, anything. Eventually, we stopped speaking to each other. I ignored him when I came home from college breaks. My parents prompted us both to say hello and goodbye.

When I got my diagnosis, something opened up, and I felt a relatedness with my brother that I hadn't ever felt before. I started speaking to him more, not about autism, but just in the way a sibling might. We had never had a relationship that was close to functional. Now, we have good conversations, and he is friends with my partner as well.

Becoming Aware of My Sexual Orientation(s): When I went to preschool, I had a best friend named Lucy. On Mother's Day, I wrote her name all over the placemat we were supposed to make for our mothers. I told my parents I wanted to marry her. My mom just sort of said, "Okay." My dad said, "Don't give her any ideas."

I became aware of my sexual orientation in sixth grade, when I idolized a certain eighth grader. I thought about her all the time. Then I suddenly thought, "Do I want to be her? Or is this a crush?" I remember specifically having a sinking feeling and thinking, "What if I'm a lesbian?" I just couldn't imagine my life getting more complicated.

Coming Out: Over the next two years, I met many friends at the Children's Theater I participated in who were gay, or bi. There was no "queer" back then. One of the girls in my year kept asking me, and I kept avoiding the subject. Eventually I told her that I thought I liked girls. When we got to high school, she told some people and eventually people knew. I didn't have to come out, everybody just knew I was gay. It was very low-key, most people at the Children's

Theater and my high-school theater group were some sort of queer. It confused a lot of people when I started dating my high school boyfriend.

I came into queerness in college. It was a new way of describing the fluidity of orientation, and of the way that one could be attracted to non-binary genders as well. I became very open about being queer, and sought academic courses and student activist groups that developed my current politics around LGBTQ+ identities.

Relationships: I have always dated whoever was my best friend at the time, and struggled to support relationships outside of that. The exception was college, when the boundaries between types of relationships became looser, and I felt I had more people that understood me and that I connected with.

I dated a boy from high school for two years. We were friends, but also just having sex. I'm still not really sure about that time. I dated a boy for about two months in the first semester of college. I became so enchanted by the weird people around me, like me. I also realized how easy it was to make boys like you. After that, I dated a girl. This was more serious and we were together for six months. It ended after her psychiatric hospitalization. I lived with two girls over the next year and had complex relationships with both. We kissed sometimes, we took baths together naked, and I had sex with one of them. After they graduated, they moved away.

I met my current partner, Violet, during my junior year of college, although we'd known each other peripherally before then through a student group. I began hanging out with her group of friends, and eventually developed a casual-but-complex relationship that eventually turned into a strong relationship. And I do consider her my closest friend. We moved to Boston together, we are both in grad school, and live together.

Our Unique Relationship: I think that queer relationships are different than traditional straight ones. My experience has been that I have changed over time, and Violet has too, but we remain very close. Our relationship doesn't hinge on or revolve around sex—we barely ever have it.

Being ASD means that Violet doesn't always know why something is wrong with me. We've been together long enough that she can read my body language and employ coping mechanisms faster than I can even imagine them. She fulfills a lot of basic needs, like making food and doing the laundry. She keeps me organized. She compensates for me. I would not be able to function if I had to devote my energy to those things, so she is the whole reason I am able to make it out in the world right now.

I am odd, and that makes Violet happy. We have our quirks and our own little language and jokes. We can even finish each other's jokes! Violet gets into my brain world easily now.

For my part, I support her emotionally in many ways. She recognizes that and reminds me how important that is to her. She tells me how supported she feels by me in a way that she does not get anywhere else. I am here for her, completely. Her recent mental illness has required me to step up and do more caring and more comforting than I usually do, which I have been able to do.

Relationship Strategies: We are both so reliant on each other for support. We communicate about everything. We do not leave things hanging in the air, and try not to go to sleep angry. We communicate clearly and explicitly, and that leads to a lot more understanding between us about things that may have otherwise gone unsaid.

When we are frustrated with each other, we talk it out until we reach a common understanding, without leaving emotions or thoughts unsaid. We recognize who needs support the most at each moment (we try not to both fall apart at the same time). We ask clearly for what we need and want and what we don't. Mostly, it's communication.

We've pursued couples counseling in the past as needed. We even went to a support group for neurodiverse couples with Eva, where we met with other couples similar to us, which was interesting and fun. However, it seemed that these couples were facing much greater marital challenges than us. We were odd as the young, queer couple in a room full of straight, mostly middle-aged couples.

Being ASD and LGBTQ+: I don't think I've ever found anyone to be informed about the intersections of these two identities outside the autistic community. Maybe a few researchers, but not the general public.

It is very tiring to live in a non-autistic world. I hit barrier after barrier. I am always tired, literally, at the end of the day, after having to "hide" myself at work, or school. The more I push myself to be out there, the longer it takes me to recover.

But I guess I can imagine not being autistic. I can't imagine not being queer. I can't imagine not being a woman. I feel that ableism has affected me enough to let me imagine this scenario. I've experienced relatively minimal challenges in life due to my sexual orientation. Being a woman is hard, and an autistic woman more so, and maybe a queer autistic woman even more. At some point, one is so far from normative society that it stops mattering and I am less able to pull these various elements of myself apart when I think of who I am overall.

Of course, being able to take a break from the world, my partner's, and my mother's complete acceptance has been most affirming and reassuring for me.

Note: See Chapter 17 for an account from Maya's partner, Violet.

Chapter 2

JO JO

I always knew I wasn't a girl, but I figured I must be, because I knew I wasn't a boy either. It was, honestly, the Internet that made me aware of my gender identity.

Name: Jo Jo

Pronouns: They/Them/Theirs

Age: 21

Education and Profession: Some college as a Psychology major

Living Situation: Currently living with my father. I will, however, be moving to live with my romantic partner very soon.

Diagnosis: High-functioning autism

Gender Identity: I identify as agender.

Sexual Orientation(s): I am bisexual and gray asexual. I feel attraction to all genders and sexes, but weakly.

ASD: I was diagnosed with high-functioning autism at age 17 and at that point it was too much of an effort to change the system I was already doing rather well in. Additionally, I was vehemently in denial about the autism diagnosis for months, until I discovered the online community and connected so deeply with the issues they were talking about. Basically Internet memes were what convinced me that the ASD diagnosis was correct.

Being Agender/Non-Binary: I always knew I wasn't a girl, but I figured I must be, because I knew I wasn't a boy either. It was, honestly, the Internet that made me aware of my gender identity. It was there that I learned of non-binary gender identities and the idea that you don't need to be either a boy or a girl. It was a quick process between learning that, and realizing that it applied to me. I identify as agender. This is based on my physical and social dysphoria. I came out to parents around age 17, and they were accepting. In a wider sense I transitioned socially after graduating high school. It can be difficult at times, with a lack of understanding and knowledge surrounding my gender identity, but I have not given up. Also, in the future, at some point, I intend to go on testosterone.

Being Bisexual and Gray Asexual: I am bisexual and gray asexual. I feel attraction to all genders and sexes, but weakly. My first romantic relationship was with a girl. It was short-lived because it was at a summer camp and we had to go home afterwards. I was 14. At 17, I had my first relationship with a boy. It lasted six months and was horrendous and abusive. My current partner and I met when I was 19 and they were 17. We have been dating ever since, and we are both bisexual, trans non-binary for gender, and somewhere on the autism spectrum, though they are self diagnosed.

Friends, Groups, and Support Systems: In the past, the people around me did not always understand the way I communicated. Now, after knowing about my diagnosis and identities, when finding a group of friends, it helps to have something in common, and both the autism and the queer identity can be a strong connector. The majority of my friends have one or both of these things in common with me.

Connecting with people who are similar or who share similar experiences is meaningful to me. I personally prefer meeting people in real life and find it more valuable than making online connections.

I was one of the founding members of my high school's GSA, which stands for Gay Straight Alliance. It consisted mostly of my group of friends. This was of course highly related to my queer identities. I also have been part of other, non-queer based communities and groups, the most recent being Toastmasters, which is basically a club for public speaking. Each week I have the opportunity to stand in front of the group and present a speech. I have performed speeches on both autism and gender. I value the opportunity to spread knowledge of these identities to people who may not have much information on them.

My partner and my family are my primary support systems. They work hard to understand and provide what I need, and help me acquire or achieve it.

Counseling: I have been in counseling/psychotherapy before. It was originally not at all helpful. I was nine years old, and refused to discuss my feelings or anything of importance. The therapist did not know how to handle this, and became frustrated with me. This first experience made me avoid counseling for a long time, even when I so clearly needed it. Finally, when I was 17, I tried once more. This therapist was more competent, but I did eventually disconnect from them. My current therapist has been remarkably helpful and I greatly appreciate how she always seemed to ask the right questions.

Coming Out and Disclosure: I suspected my sexual orientation from an early age. At first I thought that I was gay, but eventually recognized that I had some attraction for males as well. When I first came out I was 12 years old, sobbing and panicking. My family was actually quite supportive, and since then I haven't been as afraid when coming out.

People have heard of bisexual. Gray asexual and agender are new to them. I have to do a lot of explaining when I come out to a new group of people. To the point that I often exclude the gray asexual or agender aspects just for ease of explanation.

Many people mistakenly think that autistic people can't be gay because they have to be all asexual.

It seems as though a majority of people only seem to know that autism makes people unusual and not fitting into social norms, and that it is an "epidemic." It seems like many people receive their information from ableist, cure-based organizations, rather than from sources that empower autistic people. I especially feel that accommodations around autistic traits are most useful and effective.

I feel that being autistic has actually made me even more open-minded towards the LGBT community, because I simply don't understand the bigotry against them, and didn't understand it even before I knew that I fit into *that* community.

Relationships: I believe that the greatest relationship challenges come from misunderstanding. When one party does not comprehend the situation or state of the other, then there will be difficulty.

ASD and LGBT identities simply add another aspect which can be misunderstood. Though in relationships like my current one, where we share these identities, it has been a benefit rather than a detriment.

My partner and I make sure to spend a certain amount of time together away from our computers, and we ask each other what we can do to help each other. We try not to assume we know what is best for the other person.

Employment: I have lost at least two jobs because of my social difficulties. I was in a childcare position for about three weeks before I had to quit. I was also a cashier for almost a year before I was done, having it drain all my energy every shift.

Family: The most crucial aspect of my current family relationships is that my mother left our household almost a year ago. She is now divorcing my father. The second most crucial aspect would be that I am moving to Texas at the end of January to be with my romantic partner and to attend university there. My family is incredibly supportive of me. Each and every one of them listens to me and does their best to help me any way they can. My sister and I aren't very close, but we are quite amenable and when we visit each other, the interaction is positive and beneficial. My father and I are very close. We spend a lot of time together and I believe that he understands me deeply. He also works with me to help me grow and learn as a person, and to succeed in this world. I was once closer to my mother, but since she left, my father and I have gotten closer.

Note: See Chapter 18 for an account from Jo Jo's father, Fred.

Chapter 3

NIJAH

I like everyone. I don't see gender when I have an interest in someone. Like my current partner—I started liking her because I like her personality and how she carries herself. If she were male, I'd still have the same feelings for her.

Name: Nijah

Pronouns: She/Her

Age: 29

Education and Profession: Bachelor of Arts in Creative Writing. I majored in Creative Writing and English, doing an online college program.

Living Situation: I live with my partner who I have been with for nearly eight years. I love her so much.

Diagnosis: Formal Autism Spectrum Disorder evaluation/diagnosis

Gender Identity: As far as my gender identity goes, I identify as both male and female. I just feel like a boy in a woman's body at times. Growing up, I suppressed this male side of my identity to protect it from people bullying me over it. Where I grew up, people made fun of girls that appeared or acted male, claiming them to be lesbian or strange/crazy. It was pretty bad, to be honest. I do not plan to seek out medical transition hormones; I like my female body. I think the only time I get mad about being female is during my period but, other than that, I'm cool with having a woman's body.

Sexual Orientation(s): I like everyone. I don't see gender when I have an interest in someone. Like my current partner, I started liking her because I liked her personality and how she carries herself. If she were male, I'd still have the same feelings for her. So to put it simply, gender identity or sex have nothing to do with my attraction to someone. I might like their personality or how they look—them being male or female never crosses my mind.

Family: My family is not close. I used to be very close to my mother when I lived with her, but now that I'm an adult and so busy taking care of myself, maintaining a relationship with her has been difficult. However, I know she understands that I'm busy and working, and that if I had the time I'd hang out with her more. I have an older sister; I'm not close to her at all. She's probably not autistic, because she thinks I am weird and barely comes around or talks to me. At family events, I'm usually ignored most of the time; people don't really like talking to me. I don't know why, but it has always been that way for me.

I would say my mother and my partner are my supports right now. I do engage in things online and talk in forums and all that jazz, but for me, my supports are my mother and my partner. My mother wasn't the best when I was growing up because she had her own struggles, but she always tried to support me the best she could. And my partner was brave enough to approach me when most people only did it as a joke or to be funny with me.

Employment: I've kept being autistic hidden for so long that I don't think it has had any effect on my employment. However, recently, I got paperwork to submit to my job because I've been having a lot of personal issues. Now, I think that because they know I'm autistic and have proof, they may try to get rid of me. A lot of employers still don't understand how autistic employees function and think they are doing a poor job when really we're distracted. I work in a call center where there is lots of noise from the other agents talking on the phone, and I can hear all their conversations with customers. I have a hard time blocking out the extra noise and it drives me crazy all day. By the time I get home, I'm exhausted. My other employment opportunities weren't so difficult because the employer didn't know I had autism. One manager suspected I had autism because one of his children has it and he used to look out for me and remove me from situations that were causing me to freak out or panic so I wouldn't meltdown and embarrass myself. He was the coolest manager I ever had!

Diagnosis: Nobody knew I was ASD while I was growing up. Me finding out about being autistic and getting it confirmed by a professional has made me look at myself in relief and happiness because now I know where the "weird" comes from, and I'm happy. I feel my autism has shaped me into the person I am and I wouldn't trade it for anything else. Also, I kept my sexual orientation under wraps because people tend to lump me as bisexual, but I like all human gender identities not just male and female.

I think my autism has had a major positive impact on me now that I know it is there. It is a relief to know that what I suspected about myself was true the entire time.

Community: I play Massively Multiplayer Online Role-Playing Games (MMORPG) called *Final Fantasy XIV.* My character gets switched between male and female often because I like playing as both and wearing different clothes that only males can wear or only females can wear. It is a fun game with lots of content to slog through. I can say it is one of the things that gets me super-hyped. I occasionally participate in roleplay online, but not all the time. I'm a creative writer at heart, and roleplay is my other secret passion. I just haven't had as much time for it as I would like.

Counseling: My first experiences were when I was living on campus at university. I didn't do well there academically because I was struggling with a lot of things related to my undiagnosed autism at the time, so I went to see a therapist. I'm surprised she didn't pick up on the possibility of me having autism. I didn't find out I was on the spectrum until several years later at 29 years of age.

Meltdowns and Stress: During one of my recent meltdowns I was walking outside, and I literally started swinging my fists at myself and crying. I hate that my lack of understanding of communication and social things gets me into trouble. I hate that so much. It happens more often than I would like, and it always makes me look like my behavior is on purpose when it never has been or never will be. I say the things that have helped me are my passion for writing and my tendency to daydream. And when I met my partner, she became a focus for me, so I stopped hurting myself. I notice that meltdowns or the lack of coping intensifies in times of high stress. I try to keep my stress levels low.

Coming Out: I told my mother I liked everyone when I was 13. She didn't even mind it. My mother was the first person to be accepting of it, so I didn't feel a need to tell others. I did tell a close friend of mine, and she was cool about it. I didn't feel it important to tell people my sexual orientation.

I have been aware of being both male and female since I was a kid. I just pushed the male side down and out of sight because of the community I lived in. I couldn't openly show it without being bullied. It was funny really because one of my best friends in elementary school ended up being transgender and had once asked me if I would have dated them. That was back when I first talked to them after we'd had a falling out for a few years. I admitted that I would have given them a romantic chance. Of course, now that's something that will never happen. I'm happy with my current partner and I wouldn't trade her for anyone else.

Being on Multiple Spectrums: Where I grew up, people have very little knowledge about ASD. They are under the impression that people who have it are slow and can't speak. They don't seem to understand that it isn't something that children grow out of. I have seen kids that might be autistic getting screamed at and beaten in public because they're just overloaded from all their senses. It does upset me because I can tell what that child's problem is, but their parents are too ignorant to get educated and think they simply have a misbehaving child.

People aren't very educated. Most people I've run into are of the religious-nut type that will tell you that any sexuality other than hetero is sinful and that if you identify as anything different from your sex, you're going against how God made you. Since living outside of Detroit, I have run into people who are more informed about these things, so I don't have to deal with it as much as I used to.

I find some people in my hometown to be very ignorant. They are close-minded and suffocating and I feel it is best for people who suspect they are autistic and LGBTQ to look to those communities for support because even though support is available in the wider community, ignorance about autism and gender identity issues will make it difficult for you to find help.

It can be really annoying that people don't get sometimes what a struggle it can be to be autistic, especially when you're having a bad day. For me, my bad days consist of being unable to tolerate socializing with people that I don't have personal connections to, which is mostly everyone. I have zero tolerance for small talk and pointless conversation on bad days. When they're bad, I can't hide my awkwardness or dislike of socializing. I can be harsh to get people to leave me alone.

For me, my sexual orientation isn't based on what "gender" someone identifies as or is. For me, I see personalities and attractive people, not male/female. I think it is one of the things I have a hard time explaining because a lot of people don't get it. They think I'm bisexual, when really it isn't bisexuality; it is the fact that I don't prefer people based on their gender. Like in my current relationship, I am with a woman. Do I love her because she's a woman? No. I just happened to be attracted and fell in love. The fact that she's female didn't stir me at all.

My Relationship with My Partner: I have only been in *one* relationship, and that is my current one. Would I end this one and try another relationship with someone else? No. Simply because I've already put so much effort in, I would feel it a waste if I were to suddenly go, "Hey, I want to break up just so I can try a relationship with someone else." Not my cup of tea. I'm pretty loyal once someone has my attention. I just don't have the energy to pursue other people, so I am comfortable and happy with my current partner. Who needs another person when they already have the one they need?

I say the biggest strength in our relationship is that my partner is learning to understand. At first, we had more difficulty than we do now because I wasn't diagnosed and fights would happen where I didn't understand why she was upset. She wouldn't understand why I didn't seem to care. It wasn't that I didn't care, it was that I didn't understand! In relationships, a lot of things make people upset, and since my social skills and ability relating to others are pretty poor, it can cause a lot of trouble. I'm working on being better than that, but that's all I can say for now.

I'm a person who needs their alone time. I don't really get much of it, so sometimes we try to compromise. If I didn't have to work a boring day job, I'd probably be a lot happier and easier to deal with. If I wasn't working the hours when she's working, I'd spend them doing my "alone-time things" so when she came home, I'd be in a good mood and able to communicate more easily and socialize. I noticed when I'm socially drained, my poor mate has to deal with the worst of it. I try to cope by writing about the issue, talking to my therapist, or simply saying what's wrong through writing. I find my thoughts are easier to express when they are on paper. So I write to help myself cope, and I try to talk to her, but most of the time, it is really rough.

My partner was the one who found my therapist—the one who diagnosed me with ASD. My therapist went through a checklist with us and hit all the problems we were having dead-on-the-nose through the list. It confirmed for me what I had suspected the entire time.

Being Black and Advice to Others: For someone who's just discovering either their ASD, gender identity or sexual orientation—all three of these, I suggest that you take your time in telling people. A lot of people aren't friendly about these things. In some black communities, not all of them, but some, like the one I grew up in, it can be especially difficult. In my experience, there can be a lot of hate and bigotry and ignorance among black people. It can be dangerous to tell others. However, I'm not saying this to scare you. I say keep it to yourself (especially if you're LGBT) and from your family until you can stand on your own two feet without help from any of them, because the moment they find out, they may cut you off. For those who are just finding out they have ASD, I say keep going. Your family might tell you there's nothing wrong. They might sit there and try to invalidate how you feel about things. Don't let them. You can determine your own life and how it goes. Nothing people say can change you. Try to be happy with who you are.

I can tell you that the hardest thing about being a black person with autism is the ignorance amongst some people of my skin tone. A lot of them think autism is some form of retardation or that autistic people need constant care and attention. My own mother refused to get me tested because she worried about how it would make her look. I went a whole 29 years without knowing why I was different and struggled socially while girls around me excelled at it. I forced myself to socialize. For me, autism also has its benefits. As a higher-functioning autistic adult, I have a good ability to focus on the subjects or topics I love and I am able to do so without any social distractions.

It does make me feel good to know I am not the only one in this world who has dealt with such things. A lot of us have to endure hardships, and it makes us a little stronger I think.

Chapter 4

CLIFF

Mostly cis people have problems with my transness. They ask uncomfortable questions frequently, including how I have sex and the gender of my partners...

Name: Cliff

Pronouns: He/His

Age: 26

Education and Profession: Bachelor of Arts, Theology; autism support worker, waiter, entrepreneur

Living Situation: I currently live with my heterosexual, married, cisgender parents and my older (cis) sister.

Diagnosis: NonVerbal Learning Disability (NVLD), Attention Deficit Hyperactivity Disorder (ADHD); I was often put into special education classrooms for test taking. I also received occupational therapy at school and outside of it.

Gender Identity: Binary trans man

Sexual Orientation(s): Bi/pansexual

Family: My family are middle-class, cishet, educated white people. My mom has four graduate degrees, including an MBA and two Masters' degrees. My father is a project engineer. My sister is a legal assistant. There's always been an expectation of white-collar labor in my future, and I was encouraged when I chose to go to college to become a teacher. When I came out to them as trans, one of their first questions was, "How will this affect your hireability?" My family treats socializing like a chore, including with their extended family, but get really bent out of shape if I don't contact my last remaining grandparent. My sister socializes plenty with friends, but my parents mostly just see each other. Seeing friends is also treated like a chore. Going out with coworkers is a chore for them, as well. Yet they still do it if they feel it's expected.

Coming Out: I came out to myself and friends as bi in high school. It was weird, lots of awkward fetishizing by classmates. Coming out is really a lifelong thing, so I've been coming out repeatedly since then. It's much easier, for the most part, with adults, because most have some concept of being bi or pan. Some, of course, are ignorant but I'm lucky not to have to interact with them much.

I've been coming out repeatedly as trans since I was 21. I first had inklings that I wasn't a girl when I was six, but I repressed it for years. I had a resurgence of realization in high school, but again repressed it. When I was in college, I finally admitted I was trans to myself and started coming out my senior year of college. Friends were mostly great, with most of the awkwardness coming from people I'd gone to church with, since I was brought up Catholic. Work is complicated; at my restaurant job; coworkers often tell me I have to "get over" being misgendered by customers, and that I'm "too sensitive." At my professional job, people correct themselves or accept being corrected quickly.

I've been socially transitioning since 21, but it is an ongoing process. I am not out to my extended family, not concretely and not all of them.

Medical Transition: I have sought out hormones, and have been prescribed them twice. Both times, my therapy has been interrupted. First, it was interrupted by my parents against my will, and the second time there was an interruption in insurance. I have no interest in bottom surgery, but I do want top surgery.

Social Interactions When Trans and Autistic: Cis people often have problems with my transness. They ask uncomfortable questions frequently, including how I have sex and the gender of my partners; they ask about my medical transition even when I've expressly said not to. The cis are wild. I don't always want to have to be an educator when I am just trying to relax and have fun. Being trans among other trans people is amazing, like we all have this big thing in common and we're all one big family that would help each other when we need it. Cis gay men and cis lesbians can be hit or miss, but when they're good, they're great.

Overall, I am always autistic. When people treat me like a child, or they assume I won't understand something, it makes me furious. When people treat me like just another person and meet me where I am, and respect when I do have snafus, then it can be really wonderful. And again, when I'm among other autistic people, it's usually pretty wonderful.

I briefly participated in a queer rock climbing group, and will be marching with them in the upcoming Pride Parade. I do cosplay, but not as part of a group. Most of my social interactions are one-on-one, with friends who have similar interests.

Awareness of ASD, Sexuality, and Gender: People knowing about ASD is hit or miss. Many will make assumptions about what ASD means for me. Many will make jokes.

People are pretty informed about sexualities, but woefully behind on gender. People still use language like "born in the wrong body" or "biologically male/female" when these things are not used anymore for the most part. That, or people pathologize gender. "What happened to make you this way?" "Why do you want to be a man?" There are so many invalidating questions and comments that people make, they would fill a book all their own.

People aren't very informed on the intersectionality of ASD and sexualiy and gender. Or they make assumptions that people who are autistic shouldn't be able to come out or self-identify as anything but cis and hetero, because those things are seen as default settings. If I could establish a country just for autistic trans people, I would.

It's not so much about my identities, but how I express them. I like to do things like wear makeup and hair extensions and nail polish. For me, they are expressions of masculinity that isn't fragile. Sometimes people see these things as feminine only and that's utterly bizarre to me. Assigning a judgment like that to a self expression does not make sense to me in the least, and may be because I am autistic. I like to wear clothes that feel right, even if they don't always "look" right to others, because of sensory things. I like leggings and flowy tops, things seen as feminine. To me, they're just comfortable.

Another part that frustrates me is that I see cis men, particularly cis gay men, doing a lot of the things I do, and yet there's a double standard. Double standards, euphemisms, double talk, insinuations, etc. all go over my head. I will do what I want, my gender and sexuality are still valid, and the cis will have to learn to adjust.

Counseling: I have been in counseling off and on since I was young. Most of it was terrible, because I felt forced to go, felt like I had to say certain things, didn't understand why I was there, and hadn't chosen to go.

As an adult, I was able to seek out a therapist who specializes in autism and serving the LGBTQ communities. Her counseling has been invaluable, wonderful and helpful, and I've seen exponential growth in my emotional and mental health in the past few years. I can truly be myself with my therapist.

Support System: I mostly consider my coworkers and friends my support system. My parents and sister are mostly emotionally unavailable and are only minimally helpful. They always want to help on their terms, not how I need help. It is immensely insulting and frustrating.

On the flip side, my friends are fantastic—asking if and what I need, respecting when I need space because I'm so drained from life, reminding me that they do genuinely enjoy me and my presence and my personality.

My friends and therapist are amazing, encouraging, and supportive. I've learned to self-advocate and tell people when they're being offensive or invalidating or otherwise gross. I've learned which people are true friends who will stand up for me and which ones aren't, and how to identify these things in new acquaintances.

Employment: I've found that being trans is treated as a bit of a diversity card, and is generally respected by employers. My problem has been that they don't know how to discuss sensitive subjects without being too careful. On the other hand, employers have no idea how to respect and bring out the best in autistic employees or employees with ADHD, and presumably other disabilities. It's always been seen as a disability for me, so far. Because of this, I have tremendous anxiety seeking employment in my field. I also struggle with imposter syndrome, not feeling enough—educated enough or expert enough. I've recently decided to go into business with a friend and fellow trans man to create educational content on being trans and being autistic.

Romantic Relationships: I currently have four partners. I have my "significant other," an autistic cis man who identifies as aromantic and pansexual; my boyfriend, an autistic trans man who identifies as gay but dates people all over the gender spectrum; my girlfriend, a cis bi woman; and my queer platonic partner, a cis hetero woman who was also diagnosed with NVLD. I am unsure if she now identifies as autistic or not.

Many of the issues we face in our relationships, in fact most of them, arise when cishet non-ASD people, or people who are at least two of those things, are ignorant about our realities. I feel like if people were more educated they would be less terrible. However, I cannot force people to become educated or to accept me. There are also times when communication is hard because of my autism. However, there's also tremendous community in being autistic and or being trans, or otherwise LGBTQ.

I try not to date people who require me to use coping mechanisms. If I'm dating someone, I have to be comfortable enough to use self-advocacy if I have a problem.

Advice to Others: Do not be afraid to question. Do not be afraid to explore. Accept your labels, since labels give shape to the world. If you own who you are, it won't be as hard when people try to use it against you, because you have agency and strength in knowing yourself. Remembering that when people invalidate us, it isn't because we are invalid, but because they cannot handle our reality.

Chapter 5

XIOMARA

Well, I heard a person say once, "Imagine, being gay and being also autistic, that's the worst thing that could happen to anyone! Being in one minority is more than enough." I just laughed, because I think it is actually cool being Aspergay!

Name: Xiomara

Pronouns: She/Her

Age: 29

Education and Profession: College; conference interpreter

Living Situation: I live with my girlfriend.

Diagnosis: I have an official diagnosis of Asperger's/autism.

Gender Identity: I'm happy with being female.

Sexual orientation(s): Gay/lesbian. I love the female body, and I love my own body as well.

Childhood and Family: I live in Mexico. I had a "normal" childhood—at least what seemed to be normal to me. I was always shy at school and with family, but this was not seen as something strange or serious. I have no siblings and after my father died, it was just me and my mom and we really get along. I guess you could say she kinda spoils me, because she always likes to make me happy and to give me everything she is able to give me. We are a small family so I never had issues with that while growing up, no cousins, loud relatives or difficult situations, so I had a smooth and loving childhood.

Coming Out: I guess I knew I was gay since I was like eight, however I didn't actually understand what I was feeling back then, or what it meant. It wasn't until I was a teenager that I understood, but I fought it, I didn't embrace it right away. Now, I'm happy being a lesbian and it really helps that my mother is so supportive.

I came out to my mom when I was 22; well, she kinda made me tell her and she told me she knew since I was little. The rest of my family doesn't know. Well, I assume that maybe they do, but they just don't ask. Like I said, I've always been shy and private, so I don't share much.

These things are still taboo in Mexico. Although everyday these topics are becoming more natural and normal, there is still a lot of discrimination and attacks against people who are not heterosexual. And in Mexico this also has to do with the importance religion has in our society.

Employment: Some of my colleagues know about my being gay, and talking about it with them is normal. However, I try to keep my personal life private while at work. Also, I don't go to an office; I have to translate in different companies, conferences, training courses. I'm always working with different people so there are no bonds and no need to talk about my Asperger's or me being gay.

Diagnosis: I received my diagnosis sometime last year as an adult. In Mexico, I guess people are not properly informed about Asperger's in general. Talking about autism is becoming more popular now in the media, but it's not enough and it's not complete and real information. There is still a long way to go.

Social Life and Support System: I would say that I have a handful of good friends. I don't know if I want more, because not having many friends doesn't really bother me. However, I can also see how being antisocial can become a problem for finding new friends and new potential work opportunities. The few good friends that I have and that I make an effort to maintain are also gay. In college, I used to be in a musical theater group. It was the first time I felt okay with being gay and felt normal. So I could say it is good to find people that understand you and have something in common with you.

Right now, I'm grateful that my support system consists of my mom, my girlfriend, a few close friends, and the Adult Asperger's Group at the Association of Asperger Mexico.

Being Autistic and Gay: Well, I heard a person say once, "Imagine, being gay and being also autistic, that's the worst thing that could happen to anyone! Being in one minority is more than enough." I just laughed, because I think it is actually cool being Aspergay!

I'm sure many people would consider being gay and Asperger at the same time some sort of tragedy—like you have two things that make you less normal—but I see it the other way around. I just think that these two aspects of myself are just part of my personality and I don't see myself being or wanting to be different at all. I like the things that make me me.

I believe everyone deserves to live their own lives in peace, and there should be no stereotypes or levels to determine if you are normal or not, or if you are too autistic or not autistic enough, or if you are okay with your gender or not. We should just stop using labels for everything. To talk about straight people and to discriminate against them or criticize them is as bad as doing the same thing with gay or trans or autistic people. These are not diseases, they are just in our genes and the way we think, we process things, we love and we live, so they are as normal as the sun and the stars up in the sky.

I just love being me! I love loving women and being myself no matter how "gay" that might be. So I dress how I like, act the way I am and I feel quite pleased with me.

Relationships: I haven't had many romantic relationships in my life. The first relationship I had was when I was 21 and it was actually with a teacher. My other relationships were with older women as well. I guess that I felt more comfortable and preferred to be with older women because I have more things in common with them. I feel that I can talk about more things, and do more things with them than with young people, because I don't drink, I don't dance, I hate going to clubs, and don't like doing what young people do. So I prefer being around older people. My current girlfriend is just four years older than me; however, she understands me and we get along very well and respect each other. We also try to negotiate the things that might get difficult for me, like friends, going out, and social interactions.

It is difficult being in a relationship with a neurotypical, but if there is respect and understanding, you can negotiate and try to get out of your comfort zone sometimes. My relationship is strong because we talk about the things that are most challenging for me, and although sometimes it is difficult to understand me or the way I feel, we haven't had any problems or obstacles.

Trying to think like the other person is important and not just saying, "This is what I want and I am always right." You have to step into the other person's shoes and try to understand. This is a great strategy. It just requires some patience.

Advice to Others: My advice to someone who's just discovering their ASD, gender identity or sexual orientation would be to not see these things as disadvantages or obstacles in your life. This is part of who you are and they don't mean you are less good or less important, or that you are not normal. You are just different, but we all are. We don't fit into a box. We have different hair colors, height, weight, likes, dislikes, our brains work differently, our hearts feel love without asking for permission and without discriminating. And I do think that sometimes nature makes a mistake and puts a female brain and soul in a male body and vice versa, and it is normal wanting to get the correct body in order to feel happy and complete, so what I want to say is that we shouldn't be afraid of wanting to change or wanting to do whatever we want to do, as long as it makes us happy and makes us feel ourselves and in peace.

Note: See Chapter 19 for an account from Xiomara's mother, Myra.

Chapter 6

TAYLOR

I came out to my close friends as soon as I discovered/learned about asexuality, since I was thrilled to find out I wasn't "broken" as I previously thought.

Name: Taylor

Pronouns: They/Them; He/Him

Age: 23

Education and Profession: Bachelor's degree; administrative assistant, freelance illustrator

Living Situation: I live with my mother.

Diagnosis: I have an official diagnosis of Asperger's/autism. I was diagnosed as an adult. I was self-diagnosed before I received confirmation of my diagnosis.

Gender Identity: Agender—not associated with a gender; falls under the non-binary category of gender.

Sexual Orientation(s): Asexual, panromantic—attracted to all genders—however, feeling any romantic attraction is very rare.

Self-Awareness: I don't know what exact age, but around 16 or 17 (end of high school) I started to realize I was asexual. I honestly thought the idea of being "sexually attracted" to people was fake; the more we learned about sexual things in health class, the more I was personally repulsed by it. Not only did I not get the feeling, I personally found it kind of gross. As an important note, I don't view people who are sexual as gross (to each their own, everyone is different), I just personally find sexual things repulsive.

At the time, I didn't know asexuality existed—I thought there must have been something broken in how I was built, "That was it!" But I refused to go against the *broken identity* since I felt this disinterest and repulsion so strongly. If I had learned about asexuality and other sexualities/romantic attractions earlier, it would have made me more confident in my identity, and also helped combat the depression that arose from feeling so different and broken.

Coming Out as Asexual: I came out to my close friends as soon as I discovered/learned about asexuality, since I was thrilled to find out I wasn't "broken" as I previously thought. This was when I was around 17 to 18 years of age. I'm fortunate that my friends took it well, even though I knew a few of them couldn't quite grasp the idea, but they supported me regardless.

For family, I came out to my mom early in college, maybe around 18 to 19 years old. She didn't quite understand, but she tries her best to support me and respect my identity. Around the same time, my dad saw that I had liked "Asexuality Awareness Week" on my social media account. He then looked up asexuality on his own. Later, he brought it up in a conversation and I told him about my identity. He also respects my asexuality.

Harassment for Being Asexual: I have never come out to an employer or coworkers about my orientation or identity, and am honestly quite fearful of ever doing so (fear of harassment, unintentional insensitive comments, etc.). This is due to having been relatively open about being asexual in college and facing verbal harassment from others as a result. For example, a few Psychology majors tried to lecture me, saying it was impossible for a person to be asexual; I experienced the common "someone will change your mind" or people thinking I'm joking; I had sexual threats written on my dorm door when I had an asexuality flag up on it.

Panromantic: It wasn't until exploring gender that I discovered I was panromantic (although I very rarely experience romantic attraction), and came out to close friends around that time. My family had sort of begun to assume I was attracted to multiple genders, since I was out as being a member of the LBGTQ community. Both my friends and family accepted me and respected me for it, and both groups were unsurprised by this development.

Gender Identity: Around age 19 to 20, I realized that I was agender (identifying as not having a gender). Similarly to my sexuality, I knew for a long time something wasn't "right," but lacked the knowledge to identify what it was and give it a name. I remember being very young and telling my parents I wanted to be a boy when I grew up, because as a child I was taught there were "two genders," and I knew I wasn't a "girl." There was a span of a few years in high school where I tried to force myself to see myself as a "girl," which ended being bad for my mental health.

As soon as I learned about non-binary genders (genders existing outside of the binary of male and female), I felt like the part of me that had been repressed could finally express itself, and have a name. It took me a few months to settle on the identity that felt the closest to what I was, since I had been trying to ignore that part of myself for most of my life. Finally, I felt as though agender was what I felt, as no "gender" feels quite right, and it made me feel more like, well, me.

Coming Out as Agender: My friends found out pretty quickly through my less-public social media accounts. They asked a few questions to try and understand it better, and have been very supportive and respectful. They recognize that although my pronouns are different now, I'm still me. In fact, a few of my friends have questioned and explored their own gender as a result, and began using different pronouns as well. It was amazing to see my friends look at gender in a new way; many of them are more comfortable with their identities now, and we have been good supports for each other.

I am currently not out to family or anyone at work—I am afraid of how they will react to this information, since very few people know about non-binary genders. I think my sister may have found out, since I discovered she knew of my social media accounts during my time of self-discovery; however, I have not yet discussed it with her.

Medical Transition: I have not sought out a medical transition, but have considered it due to some body dysphoria. Since I am uncomfortable in medical settings, the likelihood of me going through a transition is very slim.

Asperger's/ASD: I find that most people are grossly uninformed about ASD. Many people think that having ASD means you have very obvious, intense functional differences compared to a person that is neurotypical. Many also seem to think that it automatically makes you "less intelligent." I have been told before that I can't possible be autistic because I'm "too smart," despite my social shortcomings.

In the past, I felt like my parents were disappointed by my social failures, but they have become more supportive and patient recently, now they know about Asperger's/autism.

LGBTQ+ Community: Outside the LGBTQ community, the ideas of non-binary gender and asexuality seem to be such alien concepts that most people deny the existence of the two identities. Occasionally, this may even happen within the LGBTQ community too, depending on the part of the community you interact with. I've met groups within the LGBTQ community for example who have rejected asexual individuals, saying that asexual individuals do not face discrimination and do not belong in the LGBTQ community. Of course, there are many within the community who are also willing to learn about these identities if they do not already know. Having faced discrimination for being asexual, I am fully aware of the type of discrimination present, and the ways it manifests differently than discrimination against other sexualities.

Being Autistic and LGBTQ+: For whatever reason, people tend to be baffled by this intersectionality. I have not seen many people even consider that an individual might be both autistic and LGBTQ outside of my close friend group. I have seen people try to discredit individuals saying that they have something "broken" in their brain (being autistic), which has resulted in their LGBTQ identity.

It's hard to say how being autistic/Asperger's affects my current understanding of my asexuality and gender. I do know however that Asperger's often leads me to very "black and white thinking," which prevented me from thinking "there might be genders outside of the binary" and "there might be other individuals who do not experience sexual attraction" at a younger age. It made exploring those aspects of my identity difficult, and the lack of LGBTQ information available to me growing up did not help.

Despite possibly delaying the discovery of sexuality and gender, I think Asperger's helped me pursue these discoveries once I learned of non-binary genders and of asexuality. Part of my presentation is that I take myself seriously to a degree that (I have been told) can be a bit too much. As a result, learning about non-binary identities became a "special interest," and resulted in me discovering the agender identity. Without this intense interest and how seriously I take myself, I may have never found out about the agender identity.

I have heard that there is a higher chance of autistic individuals being asexual compared to neurotypical individuals. While correlation does not equal causation, it would be interesting to see if there is a possible connection. However, I feel that it is unwise to jump to any conclusions.

Both my ASD and LGBTQ identities often have negative impacts on social interactions. Having ASD can lead me to miss or misunderstand social cues and people's intentions. This has improved as I continue to learn to recognize my mistakes, but it remains a major issue in social interactions and causes me immense anxiety.

Being LGBTQ has less of a negative impact on my social interactions, but often makes me feel like an outcast. Even though I live in a part of the country that is relatively safe for the LGBTQ community, there is always a potential danger that I could be harmed for my identity; therefore I try my best to hide it in social interactions. This creates anxiety, which can make me appear uncomfortable in certain social interactions (for example, having to pretend I am "girl" causes me a lot of mental distress, but it is almost always the safest option for me). Having to lie about my identity also makes me feel dishonest and this negative feeling can affect my social interactions without me being aware of it in the moment.

On the positive side, my ASD makes it easy to have conversations with those who share my special interests. However, if I am too into a topic, people can find me overwhelming. Finding others who have similar "special interests" is how I befriended many of my autistic friends, without even knowing at the time they were autistic.

Living in the Non-Autism Spectrum and Cis Worlds: Living in a neurotypical, cisnormative, and heteronormative world often makes me feel like I'm not quite human. Many people I have encountered treat these aspects of my identity as something scary and foreign. In some parts of the country, people seem to be openly hostile to both people with ASD and to those in the LGBTQ community.

Even in groups for ASD and LGBTQ communities, I sometimes feel like I do not belong. Within LGBTQ spaces, my asexuality and non-binary identities are occasionally scoffed at—sometimes they are not taken seriously if they know I am autistic. It is hard to find places where I feel safe and accepted, even in alleged "safe spaces."

Support System: Support from close friends and finding individuals like me have been the most affirming things for my identities and self-worth.

My close friends have supported me and learned about my identity alongside me, and have even discovered things about themselves along the way. That kind of love and support makes me feel like maybe I am worth something...if such amazing people went to such lengths because they wanted to respect who I am.

Finding individuals like me has also helped me immensely. It has made me feel less alone, and has reassured me that my identity isn't some "crazy notion" I made up (even though many people have told me that).

Currently, I have a healthy and supportive relationship with my mom, who is a major support for me. I have a relatively healthy relationship with my sister and her husband, although my sister's emotional dysregulation can make our relationship rocky at times.

I have a complicated relationship with my dad due to conflict in the past, but it is becoming more healthy and supportive.

Romantic Relationships: I have never been in a romantic relationship and am not actively seeking one out, due to fear of disrespect for my asexuality.

Counseling: I have gone to two therapists in the past. The first was a horrid experience, because the therapist told me my identity wasn't real and had to be a result of some sort of trauma. I know that even if an orientation/identity arises from trauma it is still valid; however, no trauma led to my orientation/identity. The second therapist who was an Asperger's/autism specialist was quite helpful. I went to address issues around Asperger's, but ended up in an environment that was also friendly to my identity. This made the therapy much more helpful!

Employment: Applying for jobs can result in a high level of anxiety, since it is hard to tell if a workplace is LGBTQ-friendly. I am closeted at my current job, and would like to be more open about my identity (especially gender); unfortunately my current workspace is not the safest place to be out about my gender. I am afraid to apply for another job since I worry I might find it to be similar to my current job, or even hostile to my identities.

High social anxiety and executive dysfunction also hinder the job-hunting process immensely.

Advice to Others: For anyone seeking ASD diagnosis, or who is beginning to look into it, I would suggest looking at books and websites by authors who have ASD. Also, do consult with an ASD specialist to help confirm your doubts and questions about ASD.

If you're questioning being asexual, agender, and panromantic, the best advice I can give is to pay attention to your feelings with an open mind. Pay attention to what feels "right," or most like "you." If possible, talk to individuals with the identities you may be curious about.

When talking to individuals, it is also important to keep an open mind and to apologize if you accidentally say something offensive. If you're new to the terminology for orientations/identities, it's likely that you may say something offensive. It's important to apologize when you mess up, learn from that experience, and move on. It is also important to talk to multiple individuals with identities you may be curious about, as everyone will likely have different experiences. It's all about learning and exploration, and finding what feels "right" for you.

Chapter 7

SAM

Most people also probably don't think that there's an overlap between being autistic and LGBTQ. They probably see these as separate categories.

Name: Sam

Pronouns: She/Her

Age: 39

Education and Profession: Studying for my Bachelor's in Electronic Engineering

Living Situation: Roommates. I need to share expenses to be able to afford the cost of living.

Diagnosis: I am self-diagnosed with autism/Asperger's. I've also been diagnosed with bipolar disorder and underwent treatment for that in the form of various medications. I've also had some ambiguous descriptions/diagnoses by a doctor who thought that my traits might possibly hint at ASD.

Gender Identity: I accept myself as female.

Sexual Orientation(s): Gay

Family: I grew up in a middle-class Chinese family. When we were younger both my parents worked at big companies so we were economically comfortable even though both my parents were not college graduates. We had extended families that cared for me and my brother. I went to a Chinese primary school so I learned Chinese and Chinese history/culture.

I mostly played with my brother (my sister was born later with a bigger gap between us) and we had a lot of books. I was reading at a level that was beyond my age group. I especially liked reading the encyclopedias when my father bought a set.

I never quite liked being with other children. Because most of my parents' colleagues were British and American expats, some of their children were biracial and we used English most of the time. I think most of my peers and my parents' peers who were outside the work circle considered us outsiders and my non-interactions as snobbery. I think most people find it hard to pigeonhole me.

When I was 16, my mother was diagnosed with breast cancer and later my father quit his job. Economically we struggled after that.

My father has been described by close family members as being rigid, unswerving, and disciplined. These are considered positive qualities when present in males. These traits were mostly used to describe him in the context of when he was righteous and wouldn't use his social connections to make backhand business deals.

My brother is very bright but did poorly in school. Lots of meltdowns and temper tantrums. I did too, but hid them better. Privately, I banged my head on the wall a lot out of frustration as a teenager and I think he did too, but we never talked about it to each other and I think nobody knew.

Both my parents are introverts, so are my siblings.

My mother disliked people who talked loudly or walked loudly. She has a great sense of humor, and I remember her explaining why a joke was funny by breaking it down for me. My not being able to understand the jokes was sometimes explained by the fact that English was not my first language, and they were dismissive when I had to have a Chinese joke explained to me.

Our allowances, when first given, were accompanied by a ledger book for keeping records with date/description/credit/debit/balance columns. I didn't know other parents didn't do that until much, much later. On family vacation, after checking into a hotel, the first thing my father liked to do was show us the emergency exit floor plan. Nobody thought my very formal use of speech was strange; it was attributed either to being able to use English very well or to using it poorly (rigidly) as a second language.

My sister seemed more neurotypical to me until one day she told me a story about a time when she insisted on not receiving a gift from her mother-in-law because she wouldn't be able to use it. She thought it would be a waste to take it and her husband had to tell her that it was okay to just accept the gift but that he didn't have to tell his mother they didn't use it.

I still have very conflicting emotions when I have to lie to protect someone else's feelings.

Coming Out: I came out late. I was 28 years old. Some people around me concluded, "Aha, that's why she is odd," but I think actually my "oddness" is due to the ASD. My experience of coming out as gay was mostly positive with over-compensating niceties that reflected the change of attitudes at the time towards LGBTQ people. And, of course, the fact that I was living in a liberal, progressive big city.

Being Autistic and Gay: I find the world to be loud, smelly, and too bright; and one has to follow stupid rules that make no sense.

Rain Man, Sheldon Cooper on *Big Bang Theory* and vaccines are what people think of at the mention of Asperger's. One friend told me I was a "genius/savant" because I was expressionless and not wanting to be social. She was Japanese, so her use of English was atypical in how she described my ASD traits. That was the first time I heard a very close description of ASD for me.

But usually people would "assure" me that I wasn't on the autism spectrum, as if it was a bad thing. They assumed because I was female, I couldn't be. And also, if I can make eye contact and have a firm handshake (self-taught behavior using business books), then I cannot be on the spectrum.

Strangely, I had a similar experience when I expressed attraction to the same sex. It was assumed that I couldn't be gay because I can wear a dress (when need be) and was feminine (enough). There is also a "hush-hush-I-won't-tell" attitude that I find strange. Like there is something to be ashamed of. Being in the minority does not equal bad.

I am attracted to both men and women. I was in a relationship with a cisgendered female who considered transitioning to male and did so after our relationship ended. However, I do not like to use any labels (bisexual, pansexual, queer) to describe me. While I was in that relationship I would use "gay" if needed.

Most people assume I'm straight and neurotypical. Also, this depends on the geographical location—flannel shirts and short hair are okay in the Pacific Northwest, not so much in the South. Direct, curt, straightforward speech is okay in the city, but not so much in the rural areas.

Most people also probably don't think that there's an overlap between being autistic and LGBTQ. They probably see these as separate categories.

Reading Steve Silberman's book, *Neurotribes* (2015) provided me with some understanding and insight into being on the autism spectrum. Someone had to explicitly show me examples of ASD like he did. But otherwise I don't much care to think about being on the spectrum. How do I feel about it? I already dislike disclosing myself, so I would doubly hate it if I had to double disclose. I might be okay with joining an ASD community, but am still reluctant to join an LGBTQ community because they are mostly non-Asperger's/ non-autism spectrum.

Counseling/Psychotherapy: In the beginning I didn't find counseling to be useful. Therapy was confusing and I felt like I had to fake it so the counsellor would stop pestering me. I disliked having to identify and name my feelings. I disliked having my quirks or non-eye contact falsely described as Post-Traumatic Stress Disorder (PTSD), which led me to believe that I might have had unresolved past trauma, especially when I checked out a lot in social settings to protect myself.

After I self-diagnosed, counselling became a little more helpful. It worked in a way where I made a list of things to talk about and we checked off that list as much as possible. Now, I can be myself and really say what's bothering me without it being trivialized or questioned or misunderstood.

Chapter 8

GANNON

These are some guidelines my wife and I have found useful in our relationship: lots of communication, explicitly; starting from a point of "I love you and I think we can make it work"; choosing positivity.

Name: Gannon

Pronouns: He/Him

Age: 29

Education and Profession: High school, very little college; cook—brunch-eggs

Living Situation: I live in a communal home that I share with my wife-person, our four-month-old child and my boyfriend. My wife's partner and their four-year-old child also live with us and our house is full of autistic people and fairly gender non-conforming folks.

Diagnosis: I have an official diagnosis of Asperger's/autism. As a child, I was first diagnosed with ADHD and then Asperger's Syndrome.

Gender Identity: Male; fairly blasé about conforming to typical masculine stereotypes

Sexual Orientation(s): Gay. With some wiggle-room for non-binary folks.

Self-Awareness and Coming Out: My first crush was on a girl in 3rd grade. She is one of four female-bodied persons that I have been attracted to. In 4th grade I was interested in a boy or two. It wasn't until 5th grade that I realized it was a sexual attraction. Been primarily into male-bodied people since.

During the period when I had realized that I was not straight, I was living with my aunt who is Baptist and so we were very involved in a Baptist church and following those social norms and whatnot and so it was very much a thing that I did not feel comfortable talking about or even admitting. This side of my family could be described as a combination between *The Jerry Springer Show* and *The Stepford Wives*. Once it became clear that I was gay, there was an attempt at a gay exorcism to drive out the gay demons, but of course that didn't work. And I was also falsely accused of molesting my younger cousin and kicked out of my aunt's house, which was already pretty dysfunctional. They seemed to want someone to scapegoat and blame for all the family problems.

I came out to a select number of friends in 9th grade, and to my mom in 10th grade. And over time, there's one or two cousins who I've come out to, but not the majority of the family.

My mother is autistic herself and we are very similar. She's very practical, and not traditional in her use and presentation of being female herself, so she has been very accepting of me. Also, since I was diagnosed with ADHD as a child and had an Individualized Education Plan (IEP), we've been aware that I'm not like everyone else.

My mother was in Tennessee for several years before I was born and she was a very liberal woman for the place and time. My father and mother split up when I was around one year old. Since then, I haven't really seen my father because he had moved out of the country. He hasn't really been a part of my life.

At times when I did come out, it was stressful, shameful, liberating.

Relationships: I'm polyamorous, my family consists primarily of my wife-person, our four-month-old child and my boyfriend, also my wife's partner and their four-year-old child. Our house is full of autistic people and fairly gender non-conforming folks.

My wife-person has realized within the past few years that they are non-binary rather than female. I love them, not their gender, mostly due to autistic pragmatism.

My wife and I also recently had a baby, who is four months old now. My wife and I have been together for ten years. We live together, share finances and raise a family. This might be complex to understand for many people, but being mostly gay and having a female-bodied partner has been an interesting experience for both of us. We need to have lots of communication, patience, and love. Having overlapping kinks helps too.

My boyfriend of four years and I don't live together (he lives about an hour away), which is great for our relationship in terms of having our own space; however, it is also the source of a lot of heartache because we can't always see each other as much as we'd like to.

In hetero relationships, there seems to be a set way to run the relationship in terms of social guidelines and expectations. These can often be oppressive and patriarchal. With non-traditional relationships, the individuals have to talk about everything. And communication is not a strong suit for ASD people.

These are some guidelines my wife and I have found useful in our relationship:

- Lots of communication, explicitly
- Starting from a point of "I love you and think we can make it work"
- Choosing positivity
- No rules, just boundaries
- Bravery: "Move in the direction of greatest courage" (Veaux, Rickert and Hardy, 2014)
- Treat each other honorably; do the least harm
- Constantly working on fluidity, flexibility, and respect
- I also need my own physical space and objects that provide me with comfort.

When necessary, we also pursue couples counseling with Eva, which has been helpful. Having an impartial third party has been incredibly important in seeing our dynamic. Some of the things we've worked on are tone-correcting and being mindful of how we were communicating. Also my partners have their own sets of diagnoses, namely anxiety, depression, Attention Deficit Hyperactivity Disorder (ADHD) and bipolar, which complicates things.

In the past, I've had a counselor strongly suggest that I leave my polyamorous relationships, because they were causing stress. I view this as terrible advice, but the interaction with her gave me the motivation to improve my relationships. My relationships are worthwhile enough for me to stay. Just leaving the relationships isn't going to solve the problem.

We've had differences in communication styles and me not understanding non-AS vs. autistic thinking. I often have trouble knowing and understanding what the other person is thinking, feeling, and why they are doing what they're doing. These issues have been very difficult to hash out and Eva has helped tremendously. Thank you!

Friendships: I've never understood how or why to cultivate more than one or two social relationships at a time. I felt dramatic loneliness throughout grade school and into my 20s. For the few people that I have formed attachments with, I have been a devoted and caring friend. I'll quote my friend, Laila, "You are judgmental, but in a good way. I know I could fuck up or do something bad, and you'd still support me. Because you have judged me to be a worthwhile person."

Gay Community: So far, I haven't made any efforts to be a part of any particular community. Being on the autism spectrum does influence how willing or desirous I am of social interactions and I tend to have enough people around in the house. I don't really need to leave the house because there's already ten people living in the house and so I have a lot of people around.

There also hasn't really been any particular activity that I would enjoy on a group level that I would be willing to put in the effort to do socializing. So maybe at some point, I might stumble into something that I enjoy doing with other people in that community sort of way, but as of yet not really.

People on the autism spectrum don't always fit into the stereotypical gay community. I've been fairly fortunate in who I've found as far as partners. There is also a hookup culture and to an extent it's all about having to pass as something desirable to the other person and I can definitely pass as being superficially desirable to others. Gay culture is strange, really strange.

In my experience, many gays are pretty ableist, so having a disability isn't something I advertise. At least in my age demographic, there is very much a preference for white, athletic, straight-passing gay as sort of the top of the social ladder and it goes down from there. So your sexual attractiveness number or score in large part is based on: Are you overweight? Are you straight-passing? Are you athletic? And there's this Apollo ideal. Yeah, there are a lot of problems in the gay community in terms of what we expect from ourselves and each other and what we're wanting.

Employment: Even in New York City, where I worked for almost two years, I wasn't very comfortable with myself and so didn't feel comfortable coming out at work there. Kitchens and cooking definitely are one of the last bastions of heteronormative male sexuality where the chefs are supposed to be having sex with the waitresses. It's a crude culture and depending on the people it can be either just silly and supportive or oppressive, so while I loved what I was doing, I wasn't in a rush to come out to anyone.

I wasn't out at work until I was 23 years old. I didn't really do that until I moved to Boston when I was really confident in my skills as a professional cook. Now, either people are comfortable with who I am or I realize that it may not be a good fit for me to work there. Because of this, I derive a great amount of well-being from my job, in spite of the stress it entails.

Having ADHD and ASD has been beneficial to my job! It's the combination of ADHD and autism, sort of nit-picky, high energy, wanting to keep track of multiple things all at once, while also being precise about how to pull these things off, doing more things than you possibly can. For being a line cook, at a restaurant that serves breakfast and brunch, that's very helpful, holding myself to a consistent standard of quality.

Despite having had a Mensa membership, my grouping of disabilities didn't align with college.

My choice of employment seems to have worked out for me and not going to college meant that I didn't have any college debt. Of course, there's also a ceiling for how much money a cook can make. I am considering getting some training in either electrical work or carpentry or some sort of trade of that nature. I'm good with my hands and I tend to be decent at that kind of stuff.

Self-Harming: Yes. And have done so many times throughout my life. Truthfully, reducing the stress and triggers of my autistic anxiety has helped keep the desire for self-harm at bay.

And learning to suffer productively has helped. My profession involves fire, knives, and exhausting heat, hours on my feet and sore backs and legs. Why hurt myself when my job will do that for me while I earn money and achieve goals with productivity?

I've also reduced my stress and triggers and reshaped my thinking. At some point, I caught on to the fact that when I was feeling down, if I managed to do something else like start and finish a project or go out and achieve something else that was positive and fulfilling, it would counter the desire to self-harm.

And through working, I feel like I do both: I do some suffering, but am productive where there is labor and pain involved in getting through my work day; but it's very much a structured and productive use of myself and my body.

A lot of people tend to ignore that the desire for self-harm isn't necessarily inherently wrong or to be avoided at all costs. It is obviously a red flag and in actuality very harmful, but instead of trying to work towards a point where the desire to self-harm never crosses your mind you can turn those thoughts and desires into something that's productive and healthy. It is just part of your mental makeup in terms of needing sensory feedback as an autistic person.

Raising Children: At the moment, our four-month-old child is being raised with a light default to male, but we are not putting any weight on that.

And then we have a four-year-old child, Ina, who is female-bodied and pretty consistent in not wanting to be called boy or girl. They are called they/their and occasionally it's they/girl and they/boy. Our household is by and large not very defined around gender roles.

Ina is also home-schooled, so they are probably not getting as much outside exposure. We also have another child in the household, Jayden, who is trans (female-bodied), and is very much into long hair, dresses, pink, sparkles, and whatnot. And Ina has been living with Jayden almost their entire life.

They've been around Jayden this entire time and they are living with another girl child, but Ina has no interest in dresses, pink, or long hair. They still have their hair very, very short, a touch longer than a crew cut and this is just how they prefer to keep it. It'll be interesting to see how that unfolds as they get older and more exposed to the outside world—how much of this is their understanding of the world, how much is about how the people are in the house versus who they are on a fundamental level.

ASD and LGBT: There really isn't any information that I'm aware of about the crossover between being autistic and LGBTQ, even though I believe this information would be useful. Almost all of the autistic people that I've known haven't been traditional in their sexuality.

Chapter 9

YAELI

Not long after I came out to my cousin and his wife, they mentioned that they get the trans thing, but the asexuality doesn't make any sense.

Name: Yaeli

Pronouns: She/Her

Age: 41

Education and Profession: Masters; computer engineer

Living Situation: By myself with my cat

Diagnoses: Asperger's/autism/autism spectrum

Gender Identity: Nowadays I usually just say transgender woman. It's easier to tell people I'm a transgender woman rather than going into complicated feelings. At this point I am comfortable with it, but I don't know if it's just because I've repeated it so often.

Sexual Orientation(s): I am definitely asexual but I know that there's some kind of attraction that is generally towards other women, but I have no idea if that is romantic orientation or not. That is something that I haven't quite figured out yet.

Family and Upbringing: I'm essentially by myself. My parents and brother live in New Zealand. I don't see them face-to-face that often and I have other close family—uncles, aunts, and cousins here in the States. Growing up, at one point, when my parents were in NZ, I was living with my aunt, uncle, and cousins, so even though they were technically my cousins, I considered them brothers. But lately, I don't see them that often.

I grew up in the South, but I spent a lot of time with people whose families had been transplanted Northerners or Jewish folk, so that's probably why I don't have a southern accent. From kindergarten to 1st grade I went to Hebrew school. Then in 4th grade, my family moved to the South, where suddenly, because of the private school education, I found myself to be the smartest kid in my class.

My mom did a lot of Math stuff. She was a substitute Math teacher and accountant. My dad was an archaeologist and a museum director, so we were a fairly educated family. And my grandfather maybe was a bit of a pride of his time. He was the first to apply and get accepted to college. He then chose to run a business and made money with his brothers. He was always trying to instill in all the kids the value of "You should act for the society you want to be a part of." He was keen that we knew where to put our silverware—you know the fork goes here—wear dresses or suits, learn to play tennis or golf and take business classes, so that was something that influenced me.

Employment and Socioeconomic Status: I'm sure that I've been very lucky as someone who is white and for a long time was viewed as male. I would guess that the Asperger's helped me go to MIT (Massachusetts Institute of Technology). My current employment and socioeconomic status are a result of being in the right place at the right time. My current job is at a company that my advisor started when I was a student at MIT, so I have had opportunities just fall into place.

In terms of being trans and asexual, the coming out as trans has been a more recent thing and work has been really supportive. I am lucky in this regard. I've also been really fortunate that my job is very flexible in terms of when I put in my hours, and most of the time I'm in a cube and not interacting with people. If I had to do something with set hours, I think it would be hard on my autism, so I am fortunate to have a job that fits well.

Being Diagnosed: As a child, I wasn't diagnosed. My brother was diagnosed first as he had much more emotional distress than me. As an adult, I did a neuropsych evaluation with psychologist that wasn't for AS. I was trying to explore my asexuality and was feeling lonely and started going to therapists. There were questions about anxiety and memory, so I did a battery and in the intake I mentioned that I thought I probably had Asperger's. Initially, they said, "No, you don't have Asperger's, you seem perfect." Then, they said they couldn't disprove it and that they weren't experts on it. I certainly say I have Asperger's, although lately I say autism or autism spectrum.

Friendships and Social Life: Yes! I don't know where to begin. I definitely think I don't interact normally with people and have anxiety that is probably developed from not being able to cope with the autism. I avoid people and new situations, which certainly has a negative impact. Some people think there are a lot of trans or genderqueer autistic folks just because they do whatever they want and they are not bound by gender roles or something. For me I feel like my autism meant that I just accepted whatever society told me, so it worked the opposite way for a long time. The autism made it difficult for me to be aware of my asexual feelings for a long time. Perhaps even my feelings of being lonely were because society says I am supposed to date, get married, and end up with somebody. I even attempted dating, which didn't work because I didn't quite understand asexuality and the people that I met through dating typically were more sexual. As for being trans, I think I have been lucky as I don't think it's really affected my social interactions.

Involvement in Groups/Communities: *Harry Potter* fandom played a big role in my figuring out my transness. I also started to see a therapist because I was feeling lonely and from that I started exploring my sexuality and anxiety. One of the things that they suggested that I do is start going to some meetup groups. Somehow I found that there was a *Harry Potter* meetup group and went. A lot of my friends now are people that I met there even though the group no longer meets. I occasionally go to comic book conventions now. If I had more awareness, I would have explored cross-dressing in the past, even though it might have been more like trying out genders and things that might have been more accurately me. Now, I do try to find queer and trans groups around me. I think queer-radical spaces have been attractive to me lately, so I'm trying to volunteer more with an organization called Black and Pink. It's a prison abolition organization that specifically helps incarcerated LGBTQ folks with various initiatives including pen pals and keeping contact through newsletters and support and stuff. And so I have been trying to volunteer and it has been cool to meet people through that. I've also been trying to learn Yiddish and there have been a couple of Intro to Yiddish for Queer Folks groups that I've gone to and gotten started with.

Counseling: The first therapist who gave me a concrete analysis of social interactions was very useful and I refer back to that and the coping skills people have suggested.

Being Asexual: Being asexual, I certainly didn't pursue anything sexual. It's probably related to the autism as well. Mostly because I wasn't feeling any urges to do anything, I didn't date or try anything. The first time... I think I was 25 when I happened to be at Esperanto (I should have mentioned Esperanto[1] as a community). I speak the language Esperanto and in the past I did a lot of traveling and going to conventions. Now I just go to a local meetup, occasional regional events and keep in contact with friends from when I went to my first-ever Esperanto weekend in Vermont. It was an overnight lodge thing and while there, I happened to be eyeing someone for a while and we arranged so that we ended up in the same room and that was the first time that I'd ever been like alone with someone. It was clear that I wasn't interested in doing anything other than that I liked talking and being together. There was a feeling that I might need to get over some anxiety, or that I might need to find the right person... I felt like a sense of being broken. I was in therapy, when I was probably 30 or so, when I discovered asexuality online. When I was 35 or so I went to a meetup group for asexual folks in my city, because I'd never met any asexual people before. Even though the discovery took a while, I very quickly figured out that this is probably me.

Coming Out as Asexual: Coming out to my parents was fairly easy, but I don't remember when I did that. It was mostly my mom who was always interested in grandkids, so I think at some point there was sort of a discussion that I don't think I'll be able to give you grandkids. I'm very open, not at work of course, but I am very open with my friends. When I first identified as asexual, no one had ever

---

1 Esperanto is an artificial language invented in 1887 by L.L. Zamenhof (1859–1917), a Polish physician and philologist, and intended for international use. It is based on word roots common to the major European languages (www.dictionary.com/browse/esperanto).

heard of it, and even though I wanted to be open with people, many weren't aware of it. I'm also open to people that aren't close friends just 'cause if something comes up in conversation I need to be able to say, "But wait, some people are asexual." But yeah, I don't bring it up at work. I don't know what they think in terms of a non-married person who's 41.

Coming Out as Trans and Autistic: Coming out as trans is something I remember a little more and something that was a little more nerve-wracking. In this instance, coming out has also been less of a single event. In fact being trans has been lots of things. For the longest time I thought that I was just a crossdresser, and that I would be happy doing that. For a long time, I just had this alter ego—sometimes I was Isaac and sometimes I was Yaeli. I even had separate Facebook accounts and email accounts. It was nice to have a place to share photos and statuses with the friends who knew about that side of me. At some point I figured out that wasn't enough and that I wanted to be Yaeli all the time. So then I had to come out to people. I even came out to my mom online. There I was sitting in front of my Facebook page and looking at the Send Friend request to my mom and being like, "Ehhh okay," and then I just did it. I went to bed and I don't even remember what our first conversation after that was. I came out to a lot of people on Facebook this way.

Because of my autism, I wasn't in touch with how I felt about things, so I had to figure out how I felt by doing little baby steps and then seeing how I felt and then going a little further. One of the first steps I did was just tell people I'd like to be called Yaeli. This must have been when I was around 36 years old. I also had been going to Harry Potter conventions and at the conventions there would be a ball one night. People would dress up in fancy gowns and stuff and so I used that as an opportunity to wear a fancy dress. I was being Yaeli more and more at these conventions.

Then I started reading more about genderqueer issues and began going to conferences for gender and sexuality minorities. At one of the first ones I went to, when I arrived, they handed me a blank name tag and said, "Write your name and you can use whatever name you want." That sort of like hit me like "Really? I can put Yaeli down on this and be Yaeli for the weekend and ask people to use she/her pronouns?" I had never considered that before and that was kind of like eye-opening. I was Yaeli for the weekend and I got back and realized that going back to being Isaac was kind of sad. Shortly after that I had my friends and certain family members call me Yaeli.

At first, I didn't say anything at work, but it was just getting to be too much—I'd be Yaeli everywhere else and I'd come into work and have to pretend to be someone else. I was 38 when I decided to start hormone therapy. I was a few months into that when I finally told work. I figured my changes from the hormones were going to start showing at some point.

Coming out about autism is not something I do all that often. I took time off work to be on a panel for an Autism-Trans Spectrum event and I mentioned this to work. When I returned, my boss was like, "Oh, so what is your connection to the autism part?" That's when I said, "Oh, I have Asperger's!" My boss was like, "Oh, I didn't realize," even though it seemed pretty obvious to me, and explains my irregular hours and my desire not to interact with people. So I came out as trans before I came out as autistic at work. And I don't know that I've told anyone else other than my boss but I am vocal about it on Facebook and I'm friends with some of my coworkers so I assume they see things. And I'm open about it, but I don't know how many people other than my friends know about it.

Claiming My Identity: I forget timelines now but it was in the last five or six years that I went from thinking I was a cross-dressing man, to having friends convince me to go out cross-dressed more, reading and going to conferences and it sort of snowballed into who I am today. It's taken me a long time to feel comfortable claiming my identity as a woman, because I didn't want to step into a space where I didn't share a lot of experiences, so I think that was part of my hesitation for a long time. I used to think my identity was complicated mostly because I just felt like I was still working on it and hadn't lived it as much yet. It has only been recently that people generally read me as a woman in public, so it was also very difficult to claim any of those experiences.

Awareness and Overlap of ASD, Asexuality, and Transness: Being autistic has probably affected my ability to be self-aware and figure things out. I think that I pass as neurotypical to people even though my autism seems very obvious to me because I don't often make eye contact. However, I don't need a lot of accommodation and have less need to talk to people about it. When I do come out about ASD, I definitely feel like people must have some image in their head of someone who is less capable. So they are always saying things like, "Oh you couldn't have it!" So I feel like in that sense people may not have the impressions that I would like them to have. I feel like people know something about autism, but they are not always as nuanced as I would like them to be.

I think no one had any idea about asexuality until not long ago. I find younger folks are a lot more familiar about it and, certainly in online spaces, I don't feel the need to bring it up as much because people already know or I see announcements for asexual groups and asexuality are explicitly included a lot more. I think people generally still don't have a good understanding of what it is even if they can give you a sentence definition.

As for transness, certainly that is more visible at the moment, but I think people still have a particular image in their head. There are so many experiences and ways of being trans, but I don't think that most people conceive that when they hear the word, so if I say I'm trans I'm not sure that most people would get what that is. However, there is still a way in which trans is more approachable than asexual. Not long after I came out to my cousin and his wife, they mentioned that they get the trans thing, but the asexuality doesn't make any sense.

I would certainly guess that the general public might have an impression of autism that is very infantile or incapable, so connecting sexuality or even gender to that is not on people's radar. I also think that in queer spaces there is not enough that is done around accessibility for autistic folks.

Being autistic and asexual just seem to go together so well for me, but my brother is autistic and sexual and they don't have to go together. For some people sexuality is some kind of connection to the other person in that they do something and then observe how that person enjoys that and they derive enjoyment from that. Given that I have no idea what's going on in other people's heads, the idea of having some enjoyment based on how they are feeling just isn't going to work. That just doesn't make sense to me.

Living in the Non-ASD and Cis Worlds: I think in both aspects there's a sense of alienation. I really have no idea what it is like to be other people and non-ASD. I think in terms of sexuality I probably have no clue as the things that people do when they are sexual are foreign to me. In terms of being trans, I think it is frustrating that all the typical sorts of scripts of dating and pairing up and getting married are reflective of cisgender and straight people. As such, those people just aren't forced to think about certain things or confront them, and are sort of oblivious to a lot of things. People tend to assume that trans people are doing something very different to them and that there are no overlaps with how gender and gender identity work in their own lives.

Support System: My friends are certainly affirming of who I am, and treat and accept me unconditionally as a woman. It also helps when they are conscious of autism spectrum issues and asexuality and things and are more intentional about that in the things that they say. I certainly feel the physical changes that I've done to my body have been very helpful psychologically. For aexuality I think the meetup group and community there have been helpful in terms of getting me to a point where I am confident enough to say, "This is who I am and this is the kind of life I am happy to lead and I don't have to fit into this pattern that everyone is encouraged to sort of fit in."

Having said that, I definitely need more of a support system. Certainly as I grow older, this is going to be a bigger issue. My family is pretty far away. My friends—currently a lot of my close friends I used to see—have moved, so there aren't people I can call up if I need something, for example, bringing me an orange juice when I am sick. I am fairly independent because of my Asperger's. I can think of a lot of times in my life where I did things on my own and people were like, "Oh, why didn't you ask," but also I don't feel like I have emotional needs compared to a lot of friends who are like, "Oh my god, I need to talk about this!" That never comes up for me.

Romantic Relationships: It depends how you identify relationship. I have had one or two that come close but I would tend to say I haven't been in a relationship. I don't know if I would want to be in a relationship, but I would like to try; however, it is really difficult being asexual because most people are sexual and that doesn't work for me. So I'd have to find someone that is asexual and compatible, though I don't know that I could be in a relationship and provide connection and support.

Advice to Others: One thing I realize is that people are very diverse, so I feel like any advice I would give would only be applicable to me. Try things out. In terms of figuring out gender identity for me and even asexuality, having some kind of representation was really important to realizing this is even a thing; because before figuring out transness, I thought that I was just straight and broken. I also didn't know I could be asexual. I now know it's okay to form relationships and families in different ways and so the advice I would give would just be to show people that there are more options and in terms of being trans, there isn't one way. Also, you don't have to be entirely sure to start some experimentation and voyage. You don't have to be going from point A to point B and knowing where you want to end up.

Chapter 10

OLIVIA

Being pansexual has contributed to me wanting to be a lawyer and hopefully contributing to changing society for the better.

Name: Olivia

Pronouns: She/Her

Age: 22

Education and Profession: Bachelor's of Arts in East Asian Studies; starting law school later this year

Living Situation: I live with my mother, father, and cats.

Diagnosis: I have an official diagnosis of Asperger's/autism. I was diagnosed two years ago at 20, though I had self-diagnosed/suspected it five years before my diagnosis. I also have diagnoses of mild depression and social anxiety.

Gender Identity: Cisgender female

Sexual Orientation(s): Pansexual/bisexual (I use the terms interchangeably), possibly ace-spectrum (asexual). I'm much more attracted to non-masculine people.

Family: My family relationships are complicated. My father was married before and I have three older half-siblings, each with children of their own who are around my age. One of these children, my niece, has a formal ASD diagnosis, and we suspect that another may be on the autistic spectrum as well, but my sibling has refused to have him evaluated. I have told two of my half-siblings about my ASD diagnosis, and one of them even said my niece had asked her before if I was also autistic.

I'm not very close to the rest of my father's family outside of my half-siblings and their kids, and I only see them at holidays and stuff.

Perhaps this has something to do with the fact that my siblings had a very different upbringing than me. My half-siblings had a much more lower-middle-class experience—they all dropped out of college and my siblings aren't married to the parents of their children. Now, my parents are very upper class and I didn't have to worry at all about money for college and vacations for example. Even my half-siblings' children have had a very different upbringing than me. I know there's definitely some resentment that I have such an easy time financially and that my father doesn't help them out more because of my mother and me.

My parents both believe ASD is overdiagnosed; however, they have said before that they think I may have it. That said, they are kind of against any formal diagnosis. I have not told my parents that I am autistic. As a kid, my pediatrician suspected I was autistic, but I was never diagnosed. More recently, my niece has been diagnosed with ASD, but my parents don't get it and believe it will negatively impact her career prospects.

My parents are currently going through a divorce, so right now they both are leaning on me. Additionally, my mother lost her parents and her brother passed away in the last few years, and her only remaining immediate family member is in poor health. She has a couple of aunts that are still alive in the South, who I get along well with, but I'm not out to any of them.

Coming Out: I wrote in my diary that I was bi at the age of ten, soon after learning the word. But I didn't really come out to myself until puberty, when I thought I was bi-ace.[1]

I came out to my parents as bi at the beginning of junior year of high school. I got my first girlfriend the summer between my junior and senior year, at a French language immersion camp with like 30 kids from my school, and that's how word got around to the school.

In college, I came out almost immediately.

I came out as bi/pansexual to both my parents and my sisters within the past year.

1 Bi refers to being bisexual and ace refers to being asexual.

My dad's side of the family is extremely homophobic and I don't really have any real relationship with them. I recently came out on social media, so they now know about my sexual orientation.

Being ASD and LGBTQ: Growing up, I was bullied a lot as a child. I didn't understand social cues and couldn't understand when people were being mean to me or pretending to be my friend, even when it was obvious. I tended to stare at people a lot without making eye contact, and I've managed to break that only recently. I also tend to be very honest and used to feel the need to correct people. And I kind of take what everyone is saying at face value.

However, when I reached college, I developed friendships with five close friends, about half of whom were ASD-LGBTQ people, and shared my interest in anime, so this was great! Two of them had a formal ASD diagnosis and were LGBTQ. One was LGBTQ, and another was a cishet man who shares my special interest in languages and video games. His girlfriend—also a part of the five—felt that she may be also autistic after seeing John Elder Robinson speak.[2]

People in general don't seem very informed about ASD, especially when it comes to hearing autistic people speaking about their experiences. There seems to be more awareness about sexual orientation and gender identity relative to ASD. I mean some people don't understand bisexuality/pansexuality, but for the most part I think things are changing. I think trans people have it much harder though, in terms of people understanding trans identities, even within the LGBT community.

Most of the world is just so straight though, especially those living kind of isolated in suburbia. I feel like most people don't get my friends and my interests. Like I haven't been that into anime for awhile, but I went to an anime con last year and it was nice to be around so many people that seem to "get it."

There's a definite lack of awareness regarding the overlap between ASD and LGBTQ identities, though I think it's getting better in social-justice-aware LGBTQ communities, especially with certain well-known people coming out and speaking up. Being pansexual

---

2 John Elder Robison is the author of a memoir *Look Me in the Eye* (2007), detailing his life with undiagnosed Asperger Syndrome and savant abilities, and of three other books.

has contributed to me wanting to be a lawyer and hopefully contributing to changing society for the better.

Support System: My support system would probably be my friends from college, especially one of the two ASD-LGBTQ people I mentioned. I have some other friends from college I made after we all graduated as well, and some social media friends.

I can confide to my parents about certain things, like depression, being upset about not finding a job or hearing back from jobs, but not other things. I'm still dependent on my parents. I wonder if I would be more independent were I not autistic and if I didn't have social anxiety. I get kind of overwhelmed doing tasks around the house or in a work environment if the steps aren't explained to me or if I'm expected to know to do something without being told.

I would also say getting good grades, reading, my cats and my friends/family are the things that make me feel good about myself.

Relationships: Being autistic and bi and pansexual makes it much easier to understand intersectionality, but also makes it harder to fit into the larger LGBTQ community. I don't really like bars, loud noises, or crowds (e.g. Pride), which are pretty big areas for LGBTQ people to meet other LGBTQ people.

I dated my first girlfriend for a few months when I was 16. We met at a French language immersion camp, and that kind of led to me coming out. I tried to hide my relationship from my parents, but it didn't work. My mom wanted me to break up with her, my dad never said anything about it. After a few months, I withdrew from my girlfriend socially—she wanted to talk all the time and I wanted alone time, and she wasn't having her emotional needs met. She asked to take a break after another girl expressed interest in her, so I dumped her. Looking back, I was pretty cold to her. We kept in touch sporadically because I was getting bullied by a gay guy who went to French camp with us, and he was saying some pretty awful things about her too, even a year later. And I let her know about that. But she and I are no longer on speaking terms.

I tried dating one of my close lesbian autistic friends my first year of college. It lasted a week; it was pretty funny looking back. She and I are still really close, and I'm so lucky to have her as a friend. It's probably the closest relationship I have in some ways.

I hooked up with a guy I met on a dating app a few months ago. He was one of the few guys I've found attractive and we went on a date. I hooked up with him because I was a bit embarrassed about being a virgin at almost 22 and I wanted to see what it was like. It was pretty boring, not bad, but just not for me, and I misread him and I was more looking for a friend afterwards while he was looking for a one-night stand. It made me question if I was actually ace for a bit again, but I'm still more comfortable with the term pan or bi. There are a few masculine people I've been attracted to (even though I'm mostly attracted to non-masculine people) and I think bi or pan suits me better than ace.

Communication and understanding what a partner needs is important in any relationship. I've failed with that before in both romantic and platonic relationships. I think it's very important that everyone be honest with each other and understand each other's needs and boundaries.

Chapter 11

MARIO

My sister is queer as well, and out to the family. I am not out except to her—it just has not been a necessity since my primary relationships have been with female-identified people.

Name: Mario

Pronouns: He/Him

Age: 41

Education and Profession: Bachelor's Degree; IT information security

Living Situation: I live with my girlfriend.

Diagnoses: Self-diagnosed autism/Asperger's

Gender Identity: Cisgender male

Sexual Orientation(s): Pansexual/queer

Being Autistic/Asperger's: I was born in 1975 and grew up in Spain, just after Franco's four-decade dictatorship ended. The country had relatively few means and was trying to catch up with the rest of the world on science, education and various other fields of endeavor. I attended a very good school, and from early on the teachers and staff there knew I was different. The problem was they did not know how—I don't think knowledge of Asperger's was prevalent in the late 70s/early 80s. So the school attempted various different programs and accommodations for me, but ultimately ended up leaving me in regular classes.

My Asperger's can present some tricky aspects of social interaction. Growing up I became very aware of my complete inability to read people—their expressions, tones of voice, feelings, etc. It took a long time to adapt to that and teach myself how to do it. Even as a well-functioning adult (I believe!), if I am overly tired or very distracted I can absolutely miss those cues.

While I do not know this for certain (as I have no other experiences to compare to), I credit my Asperger's with some of my tendencies towards logical thought and systems-oriented thinking. This helps with my IT security career quite a bit, as I can often troubleshoot or figure out problems and see consequences faster than many others.

I've also found it fairly easy to "step outside myself," so to speak, and think about things rather dispassionately. I hear this is not entirely uncommon in Aspies. In a way this has helped me understand how other people can be different, whether in terms of their orientation, gender identity, or thought processes.

While more and more people are becoming familiar with autism/Asperger's, many people are still not very familiar even about the existence of high-functioning autism! I have met a substantial number of people that identify as Aspies in the kink and queer communities, and I find them to be more knowledgeable than the general population.

Straight-Passing Privilege and Pansexual/Queer: While I identify as pansexual/queer, my primary relationships have been with female-identified people. In addition to being with female-identified people, I've been attracted to male partners from a very, very young age. I am only "out" to my friends in the kink and queer communities, and my sister, who has been dating exclusively female partners for years.

I am keenly aware though that I have "straight-passing privilege" and so I do not believe that I have had to deal with any negative effects of my being pansexual/queer either in the workplace or with my family. I live with a female girlfriend, whom my "vanilla" friends/coworkers and family members are aware of; however, I do not discuss my polyamorous relationships with them.

I am "out" in the kink/BDSM/queer scene, and being pansexual or queer in that environment is very accepted. In the kink and queer communities, there seem to be enough people that are aware of non-conforming populations that it's almost normalized. Then again, in these communities, different is good.

Family: I have a great and very supportive family. My core family consists of my mother, brother, and sister. My sister is queer as well, and out to the family. I am not out except to her—it just has not been a necessity since my primary relationships have been with female-identified people. I am the only one of my siblings with a college degree. Culturally we are very European, socially liberal, and yet old world.

My family was active in the diplomatic world, so I had plenty of good examples to imitate social skills from. I tend to get a lot of passing privilege as I'm socially well adapted due to my upbringing, so my social skills aren't as bad as they might have been for someone who didn't have this type of exposure.

I had a tougher time growing up in Spain, where it was clear I was different from all other children, but they did not know how.

My family is in another country, so these days my primary support system are several close friends and some in the kink and queer community. Finding acceptance and understanding in my partner and friends, who are in many ways my family of choice, has been most affirming to me.

Relationships: I have in the past dated monogamously for many years, until a few years ago I met a partner that introduced me to polyamory. I have never been a jealous person and was only monogamous out of social habit rather than any real conviction. I currently live with my girlfriend and we both have multiple other relationships—some long-standing, some just starting.

I think that every relationship has challenges. Every letter in the LGBTQ+ alphabet soup has it's own unique challenges to face, as do AS relationships.

In my own experience, having dated straight people, they were not very keen on bi/pansexual partners as they could feel jealous of their partner being attracted to people of the same gender, and not just the opposite. In my Aspie experience, I've found that some partners lacked the necessary flexibility to understand that different wiring leads to different results. I am very lucky in that my current partner is queer and experienced with Asperger's. She may not be neurotypical either, but has never been diagnosed.

In my relationships, I find that communication is crucial, as open and clear as possible. On occasion, negotiation about communication has also been necessary to establish how to best talk to each other in terms of styles and triggers.

Advice to Others: I'd recommend learning about yourself as much as you can, and helping any close people in your life (whether romantic partners, siblings, parents) do the same. There is good material out on the Internet (don't trust everything you read though!), and there are many that have very helpfully shared their experiences and thoughts. Understanding why some of your own behaviors happen is useful in preventing or controlling them, especially if they are disruptive. Alternatively, using some of positive traits to your advantage is also a good thing.

Chapter 12

PHOENIX

Culturally, many Hispanic parents are ignorant and uninformed and don't believe in ASD or LGBTQ, sometimes going as far as being violent about it.

Name: Phoenix

Pronouns: They/Their

Age: 24

Education and Profession: College student; Major: Art/Animation

Living Situation: I live with my dad, step-mom, sister and step-brother. And of course, Gnocchi, my cat.

Diagnoses: Childhood ASD. However, my parents refused to seek help. Depression. Anxiety. For two years in elementary school, I was in a remedial reading program.When I was 11, I had mandatory child therapy because of my parent's divorce. And in high school, I had therapy again.

Gender Identity: Agender and non-binary. I also identify as trans.

Sexual Orientation(s): Asexual and sex-repulsed

Family: I come from a poor Hispanic family. My mom and dad never had the chance to finish college. Culturally, many Hispanic parents are ignorant and uninformed and don't believe in ASD or LGBTQ, sometimes going as far as being violent about it. My parents don't acknowledge any of my identities, wishing to view me as a "normal cis adult" so I don't bring shame on them or our family. I have a better relationship with my siblings, but they also don't acknowledge me, refusing to use my preferred pronouns. I had a very violent, negative, and abusive upbringing, to the point my therapist has said I've blocked out most of it for my own self-preservation. I've always lived my life poor, but with most of the basics.

I have always been very different from my family. I can't remember how many times I asked them if they felt like I do. It became very clear to me that I'm different, especially after high school. Nothing made sense until I looked up how I felt. My friends have also been a little different from the norm so that also helped as a way to see where I stood. For my self-worth, it was clear to acknowledge how I felt about myself.

Being ASD and LGBTQ: People tell me rude stuff and don't take what I have to say seriously. I can't trust most people so I don't show my true colors to them and stay at an arm's length. My parents deny this reality.

Most people are misinformed about ASD to the max. Many peers and even my own family deny the possibility that I could be autistic because they think I'm too smart! I'm not sure what the deal is with mainstream society, but only acknowledging the "tell-tale signs of autism" is ableist.

Most people tend to ignore that I am asexual and agender since I don't present myself as androgyne as possible. So, it comes as a surprise to them and I must keep reminding them.

People are also misinformed about the intersecting identities. There are a lot of misconceptions and an unwillingness to listen, especially for autism and the BTQ part of LGBTQ. I don't think that being autistic has influenced my understanding of sexual orientation and gender identity. To be frank, I have a good understanding about this. But I can't be sure how being autistic and BTQ has affected me. Everyone has a different experience, myself included. I like being autistic and LGBTQ because it explains who I am and partially who I choose to be. I've come to terms with it.

Support: Birds of a feather flock together. Many of my friends also have non-conforming identities, which has brought us closer. Sharing something in common has also helped build trust and bonds. My friends know that I love them as they are and will not deny them their identity. My friends are my support system. So are my sisters, my campus mental health offices, college professors and therapists. Recently, a college professor reached out to help me as well.

Groups and Communities: I also volunteer for Latinas for STEM (science, technology, engineering and mathematics). I like cosplaying with friends. I'm also involved in some art collaborations with friends. Recently, I applied for my school food pantry, so that's also a thing. As a Latinx student, I enjoy working with young Latina students to help them reach their potential. I really enjoy cosplaying because I get to explore makeup in a way that doesn't immediately mark me as a woman. Also, it's a lot of fun to be with people who acknowledge my identities. The food pantry also gives me the chance to work with other LGBTQ students.

If I were in a romantic relationship, I believe there might be unique challenges. Being different and a minority come with resistance from others. But I've never been in a relationship, so I'm not sure.

It can be exhausting and depressing living in the non-spectrum and cis worlds. I can't express myself fully without being reminded that they don't like autistic or trans. I know people are really trying to understand the situation, but I can only be myself around my friends and circle.

Counseling: I've been in and out of therapy since I was 11 years old. As a kid I felt like therapists wouldn't listen to what I had to say. In 2013, just as therapy was starting to work, I grew increasingly paranoid about sessions. Recently, in 2016, therapy has been extremely helpful. I've been able to resolve some of my issues growing up as a kid. My current therapists are also more informed and far more accepting of who I am as a person.

Coming Out: I was really young when I came out. I can't remember exactly when I came out to myself, but probably after high school. I've never liked being with anyone, so I've always been kind of aware of being bisexual for a while. I came out to my friends in high school. My friends knew as soon as I knew. I came out to my family when I was in college. I thought my parents would try to understand me but I was wrong. My friends are supportive, but my family is rude and angry. I honestly don't tell coworkers. I've only told one coworker about a year ago. He's pansexual, so it made sense. It went well. My friends have been nothing but supportive.

I don't plan on seeking out a medical transition. I'm good the way I am.

Being Hispanic: Yes, my experiences are different because of my cultural background. Being transgender and LGBTQ is viewed negatively and there's a lack of education for these topics. Especially for Hispanic women, there is a lot of pressure to stay in the closet. I can't say for sure how different this is from other cultures, but in comparison to white American backgrounds, it is different. As far as ASD, it's almost a forbidden subject in Hispanic culture. It's not viewed as something to talk about and there's heavy shunning for anything relating to mental health and autism.

Advice to Others: Do research and learn about it. It's good to learn more and not stay in the dark. Learning about yourself is a rewarding experience. That's how I learned to stop hating myself for being different. Do this for yourself and no one else. But most of all keep yourself safe, I can't stress how terrible it can be to be at the mercy of someone who wishes to harm you for being yourself. Sometimes I have had to choose my safety over my freedom to express who I am.

Chapter 13

SILAS

I'm fully aware of existing gender conventions, but I don't want to use my body as a canvas for how society thinks. Gender roles are not biological and I am not forcing my views onto others by wearing a dress. I'm just trying to be myself.

Name: Silas

Pronouns: He/His

Age: 28

Education and Profession: Bachelor of Arts; musician, educator, artist, computer technician, adventurer

Living Situation: I live with both of my parents.

Diagnosis: I have an official diagnosis of Asperger's/autism. I was diagnosed as a child with AS and OCD.

Gender Identity: I'm a cisgender male but I am more comfortable wearing a dress, which I have done non-stop for the last year and a half. Thus, I am what some call "gender non-conforming," for lack of a more objective and less insulting word.

Sexual Orientation(s): Various

Coming Out: I tried to come out with my gender expression at different ages but felt like I was pushed back into the closet each time. However, for the past three years, I haven't stopped trying to come out.

I'm not an object. I'm not something that you can throw clothes on, especially not because of my gender. I'm too old now. I'm over 18. Even a three-year-old can dress themselves, so why can't I? Right now, I couldn't care less about what people's gender expectations are.

Being out as a man in a dress is extremely challenging. Internally, I feel healthier. I'm eating better. But externally, people are talking behind my back. People who know me say that I'm not being myself when I wear a dress because they don't understand how wearing a dress influences me internally.

Also, there's a lot of negativity and discrimination online. I even came across a Nazi comment that calls for "Hitler to come and exterminate trans and dykes."

Girls: Around ages 11 or 12, I became aware of being attracted to girls. I was unaware that other kids also felt similar attractions to others, so it felt embarrassing to feel this way. That is, until we were all 13 years old and these feelings of attraction were normalized.

Employment: Unfortunately, I was fired from my job for being a man in a dress. I met the requirements for becoming a permanent employee, but when I wore a dress the next day, they took me into a room in the back and put me on a 30-day extension for temporary placement for not doing my current job well.

My parents really wanted me to keep the job, so they asked me to stop wearing a dress. They even threatened to kick me out of the house. Since I didn't want to risk losing the roof over my head, I did everything I could to stick with that job. However, after the 30 days were up, they fired me anyway.

I feel like I was discriminated against by this company; however, legally I don't have any proof to present to a court of law in this regard. I have had no paid employment ever since.

Family: I have my parents and an older sister who is more than a decade older than me. Since I've been trying to come out for the past three years, my family has been trying to support me in every way that they understand. However, they do not acknowledge the sexism (and humiliation) that occurs when society doesn't accept one gender wearing dresses. I am glad that they still let me wear dresses around and outside the house.

Why I Wear a Dress: I've wanted to wear a dress ever since I can remember. When I was like four or five years old, I tried wearing dresses, but my parents pushed me back into the closet.

Then, about three years ago, I saw a video about Jazz Jennings, a transgender youth, social media personality, and the author of *Being Jazz: My Life as a (Transgender) Teen* (2017). It occurred to me then that I'm not really that different. Even though I'm not trans, I can still wear a dress.

Wearing dresses improves my overall performance. It makes me feel my best. I feel emotionally well. I just feel better in a dress. If you asked me how I discovered wearing a dress makes me feel good, I'd say, "Women put on dresses and they discover that it makes them feel good, don't they?"

Wearing a dress just makes me feel better mentally and emotionally—the way a woman might feel in her prettiest dress, or a man would feel good dressing smartly in a suit; basically, something that enhances their overall feelings of well-being.

I'm fully aware of existing gender conventions, but I don't want to use my body as a canvas for how society thinks. Gender roles are not biological and I am not forcing my views onto others by wearing a dress. I'm just trying to be myself.

Social Impact of Wearing a Dress: I've never really had consistent acquaintances or friends in my life. Depending on how old I was, I've had different people around me, which was mostly due to my ASD. When I was younger, I received occupational therapy, saw a psychiatrist, received behavioral therapy, and worked with other paraprofessionals—all of whom were for my ASD and OCD issues.

In school, I had a group of friends for one year and then I went off to a few different social groups. I received some support in college as well from Student Disability Services. Before and after the job I got fired from, I also volunteered at various positions where I interacted with a number of people. Unfortunately, my social life right now is very dull because of my wearing a dress.

I do attend an Expressive Arts Group at my local Asperger's organization and am part of an orchestra in a neighboring town—neither of which has anything to do with my identity of course.

Support System: Currently, it's my parents and two psychotherapists.

Counselors: I've found therapy to be mostly useful. I have been in therapy for a long time, I can't say exactly how long—since I was a child. I currently see two counselors. I don't feel like my therapists are completely able to understand my gender non-conforming experience. However, when I was trying to come out, they really helped me by speaking with my parents, who were trying to make me wear pants. Because my counselors were able to support my gender expression, they also helped my self-worth. I'm really grateful for this.

Medical Transition: Having a medical transition did occur to me, but not any more. I did experiment with my identity to see if hormone replacement therapy was necessary.

Asperger's/Autism: Autism gives me the ability to think outside the box. That said, there are certain organizations that advocate for an autism cure, and there are those who fear that vaccines cause autism (which I doubt). I think people are not informed enough about ASD.

People I know say that my wearing of a dress could be "Aspergery." Autism doesn't stop me from knowing what the gender norms are. Personally, I do not see how AS/ASD and being LGBTQ are related.

Chapter 14

ANNIE

Being lesbian and autistic are me. I like me! It's easier to negotiate the world once you understand who and how you are.

Name: Annie

Pronouns: She/Her

Age: 50

Education and Profession: Bachelor of Arts; Bachelor of Science; software engineer

Living Situation: I currently live with my wife and adult son.

Diagnosis: Formal autism diagnosis

Gender Identity: Female

Sexual Orientation(s): Lesbian

Family: My mother is also a married lesbian. My family is very liberal and accepting. My father is also an engineer. He loves interesting ideas and has always been unconditionally supportive. My sister is heterosexual and married with three children. She is a high-powered lawyer and her husband is a stay-at-home dad. The women in my family tend to be the ones who take initiative in starting relationships, and are the main breadwinners. This has given my son some interesting challenges, but he seems to have come through it very well. One of the challenges he and I have discussed—only later in life, when he was an early adult—was how I (and his father as well) raised him with a lot of skills on how to be an introvert, but he is an extrovert.

Being ASD and a Lesbian: I didn't figure out I was gay until I was in my early 30s. I often thought people were uncomfortable around me until they understood my sexuality. This process was repeated with my autism diagnosis and it has made things vastly easier. I don't worry about things anymore. The biggest change actually came when I figured out, at 30, that I had to smile at people. That was not my normal state, but I was able to train myself until it was natural. I wish it hadn't taken me until I was 30 to figure it out, but it did.

Perhaps because of my ASD, I am very anti-group. All my hobbies are solitary. Seeing my same friends a few times a year is plenty.

Once I found myself around lesbians, I immediately felt happier and more accepted. My life became much better in numerous ways. With such a broad spectrum of masculinity and femininity, I fit right in. I also discovered I only glam out and wear makeup and jewelry when I am to be around lesbians. I feel quite uncomfortable in this attire in the straight world. It's a piece of gender identity that only occurs in a limited context, but that makes it fun.

People aren't very aware of ASD overall, but everyone knows about gay issues these days.

Coming Out: Once I figured out I was gay, I told everyone. It was a "yahoo!" kind of thing. My mother was delighted, my father supportive, as was my son who was eight years old at the time. I didn't have any friends I think. My future wife's friends and family welcomed me with open arms.

I have one or two coworkers who I think were negative about it, but the company is very clear about people who are diverse. They are not just to be tolerated but to be treated with respect and inclusion. Others have made a point to tell me good wishes. My younger coworkers look bored, perhaps because these things are not shocking to them and they might have also grown up with LGBTQ peers.

About the autism, I have not told very many people. My family has been good about it, although my mother was kind of horrified. My father thought it was very interesting, my sister was supportive, and my wife was glad to have her observations explained. When we told our friends, there were a few questions, but they were cool about it. I told two people at work who I thought needed to be told. They have been fine; one of them turned out to have an autistic daughter. I thought, "No wonder we've always communicated so easily."

Acceptance from key people makes me tear up, so I know I care.

Being lesbian and autistic are me. I like me! It's easier to negotiate the world once you understand who and how you are.

Being Married: I had a husband for 13 years; we moved in together when I was 18. The first four years were great. He became very distant sexually after I had my son. He remained my great friend though until long after the divorce. I was just getting ready to initiate the final separation of that marriage when I met my now wife. We moved in together six months later and are still together. My wife and I are very close.

I don't understand many aspects of people's relationship problems. I have always known who to trust, although that is truly rare. I feel like this relates to the autism. I see different things than other people do, and I can spot fakery a mile away. Other things I am limited in perhaps. I feel like my wants and needs are very simple, but I have a low tolerance for conflict and drama. This was a negative in my first marriage. I think people who have less support from their family/neighbors/friends about their gayness have relationships that are more stressed.

I did learn that it's okay to have conflict when I am angry, and not speaking up is worse in the long run. My wife is very skilled in relationships and people generally. She really appreciates my steadiness and consistency. I don't stop loving once I love and I don't think of tricky sorts of things, so I am very predictable. I enjoy her being able to figure stuff out where I struggle. We have nearly opposite skill sets, so we make a great couple.

A good example is how we are as dog owners. I am very good at the stuff most people hate. I love to walk the dog every day and don't mind the giving of pills or other medical tasks or picking up the poop. My wife loves the training and the ensuring of the dog's emotional happiness. She knows when the dog is unhappy and needs something. Together we provide a great environment and all three of us are happier together than any of us alone. I have been heard saying, "I don't know what the point of my life is, if it is not to make my dog's life better." That's only partly true.

Counseling: I remember being 16 and standing in the shower crying hysterically. I had one short moment where I knew I was thinking suicide in the back of my brain. But, I wrapped my arms around myself and told myself I would always be there for me.

I went to counseling because I was very depressed as a teenager. Nothing made sense. I still don't know what it was about. Something about school was exquisitely painful. This was the same for my son also, but he is not autistic. Later in college I went to counseling twice. The first time, I was struggling with stress overload. Later I was getting divorced, coming out, and realizing I needed to change my major, so I was again stressed out.

Later I started to realize I was probably autistic, and then it became necessary to be diagnosed for my job.

Lesbian Socioeconomics: Being an engineer, I have been able to gain a well-paid, stable job. I think it is likely that my autism is part of why I became an engineer after about a 20-year journey of figuring who I was and what I liked. My mother had me convinced in the beginning that I liked management. It took a long time to gain the understanding that I have zero interest in jobs that are excessively "people-y." And I love Math. I enjoy my job and play a key role there. I am part of a group that respects my technical skills and we can also enjoy each other's company.

As a lesbian, I wince at how much more I make than any of my friends. Older lesbians in general do not seem to be well-off. I don't know enough to speak for the young ones. I hope they are doing better.

Chapter 15

ALYIA

Being trans, you get a lot of assumptions across the board. People are curious, asking personal questions: "Do you like binary girls or boys, or did that switch all of a sudden?"

Name: Alyia

Pronouns: She/Her

Age: 39

Education and Profession: Bachelor of Arts in Interdisciplinary Studies; semi-retired arborist (International Society of Arboriculture certified); currently underemployed. Teaching myself welding and electric wiring; too poor to enroll in classes.

Living Situation: For the last several years my housing has been far more variable then desired: a series of short-term, economically necessary arrangements, consistently lacking in well-cleaned common spaces. It's emotionally exhausting, having to compulsively care for such places. I currently live with one housemate, who is not very friendly nor of my choosing, but this is better than the almost 30 people I was living with at a housing collective last year.

Diagnosis: I have a formal ASD diagnosis.

Gender Identity: Female, Tankgirl,[1] trans, queer

Sexual Orientations(s): Lesbian, queer, bi

1 Definition of Tankgirl as per Alyia: Tankgirl is a comic book character. Basically, Tankgirl is kind of feminine but not high heels mode; more like combat boots and armament and lipstick. Tankgirl is a non-conformist who doesn't fit into female gender roles of society, "You're female so therefore you should be subservient and whatever else is on that standard list for expected behaviors." Nope!

Family: My parents live together in a wealthy-bubble-seaside-New England town. Mom's awesome! She's the only one who comes to visit me. Dad's on the other side of things: trying to adjust to the present. Formerly, one of his biggest regrets was that he didn't have a better relationship with his firstborn son, as opposed to my little brother. My dad has always had a good relationship with his *only* son—my little brother, who works for the government and is married. My brother's got a child, two houses in two different states, and a good job. So I am held up to that ideal: "If you could just apply yourself, then you could do these things in the world, as opposed to just barely making food, rent, and keeping a car from getting repossessed." My mom is the only one who understands my economics, probably because she grew up in a poor family. She's also on board with everything gender-wise.

Even though we are siblings, my brother and I talk maybe a couple of times a year—without any antagonism towards each other. I'm closer to my friends than I am to my brother.

Socioeconomics of Being Trans: It takes a lot of effort for me to remember to get the right clothing, the cookie cutter outfit that suggests that I'm in the same boat of normalcy as everybody. I am always wearing climbing clothing and that works really well in the tree work community. So when I'm not working in that area as much any more, people wonder why I wear outdoorsy clothing. Like when applying for a job to stock shelves at a grocery store, I don't have the right clothing and am not always comfortable wearing the proper clothing.

I have sensory issues with clothes, so jobs that have company-dictated uniforms or outfits, unless that actually works with me, are a guaranteed no. Now, due to my top surgery, which has made it obvious that I don't have a standard cishetero upper body, I've had a lackluster time getting employment in the tree work community here unless I get direct work from the clients. Most of the companies won't hire me full time; and after surgery, companies that I had pre-arranged agreements with stopped calling back. This is odd because most of the clients really liked me and the fact that I didn't approach everything with a "Let's kill it all" attitude. It's almost like I'm the safe person to talk to. It is the expectation of how clients will react that the companies seem to be afraid of, not actually the average client's reaction. Down South, where I live now, more so than in the Northeast, arborists are like gladiators in the yard trying to kill with chainsaws.

Impact on Social Interactions: There are people who want nothing to do with you in the world because of either presumed or actual LGBTQ identity. Then there are other people that take a look at you in line in the grocery store and smile at you and I feel like the unspoken message is: "Yeah, we just haven't met yet social circle-wise, but you're going to be okay to talk and interact with."

A few years back, I was excluded from a certain social circle based on false perceptions—I was seen as this stereotypical chainsaw-wielding individual based on my physical appearance, so they felt I wouldn't be supportive at all of who they were. So sometimes, depending on how you get ID'd, you can be excluded from one group or another. I was once told I couldn't stay at a trans household while traveling because apparently my clothes were too paramilitary (an outfit I default to when traveling because it's my favorite thing to wear), and perhaps my speech pattern and recognizing things socially were off due to the Aspie side of things. Both Aspie and LGBTQ have had both positives and negatives in social interactions.

Some people are comforted by my being there; they correctly assume I'm not going to judge them for being LGBTQ. Then there are other places, where I might be the one representative in that social group, which has people using me as a frame of reference. That's been huge part of my experience: that you can make a whole room uncomfortable just by being there and people throwing preset ideas around.

Sometimes I'll get invited to things socially and if I don't know enough people there, I'll just decline. It'd be almost ruder to show up and then realize that you're a public spectacle and leave right away—that doesn't look so good for the person who invited me. Even though my friend may want to hang out with me, it's their friends who aren't very hospitable. Not intentionally, just folks that would rather know your birth name, constantly misgendering, stuff like that. That could sometimes derail me for a whole day. I don't want to always to be a full-time educator for folks who can't use Google.

In the community that I live in now, enough of my friends function as mutual support, so usually if somebody's off on something interaction-wise, they pull that person aside and say, "You really need to work on that." It's a large reason why both my partner and I are here. Our community is higher than average in social awareness of all kinds: gender and social structures. Also, the degree of background tension is much reduced here, so much so that if I have to leave for a few days, the amount of back and muscle tension just starts to build up on me. Economically, where I live now is not a good place for me, but in other ways this is a much healthier place for me to be.

I've adopted friends as family. And I have my biological family for better or worse. Overall, my mom is supportive and all of my friends really like her. My friends would tolerate my dad. But he has a hard enough time with pronouns that I don't feel introducing him down here would be comfortable for anyone.

Groups and Communities: I interact with a lot of people who are into cosplay and gaming communities. I'm not explicitly a part of them myself, but I feel welcomed in their community. I spent a lot of time doing theater when I was younger and more than 50% of the individuals I was interacting with were LGBT or queer. I tried playing Dungeons and Dragons once at the request of a friend; it didn't work. I was in a room full of teenage boys and it left me crying most of the time. I have since met up with some queer and trans gaming groups that I've liked. I just haven't reached out much socially in the last half year due to my medical transition.

Counseling: We—Eva and I—have had some good sessions. A number of my friends down here work in the counseling field and it's a really good supportive community where a lot of things can be discussed. When I was young, I got stuck being sent to counseling because I wasn't doing well socially and wasn't getting along with my dad. Those were usually pretty lousy trips. Eventually I ended up with a parent of someone I went to school with. He said to me, "Okay, it's been explained why you've been sent to me and you're not any weirder than my kid is. Unless your dad is willing to come in as well, he's hiring me to make himself feel good because there's nothing I can do with you. So we should play chess and you can ask me questions about psychology and learn something while you're here." That was a good experience.

Generally when I was younger, I couldn't talk about much about gender. From my speech pattern or whatever, some counselors assumed I must be gay and must be in the closet about it. I had to become more honest about myself to avoid being pigeonholed in counseling. The individuals I ended up with in the past were lackluster as a whole.

Coming Out: It's been a gradually-over-time thing: realizing there was a disconnect on a few different levels. As a child, I was often in my own little world and mostly just did what I wanted and didn't understand why that didn't work very well. When I was elementary school age, I didn't understand why I was excluded. At certain points I'd want to play games and do activities like running around and climbing over things that mostly just the boys were doing. I had an interest in dressing Barbie dolls, and wondered where all the missing female GI Joe action figures were. I may have been better at social interaction if I'd done more roleplaying at a young age, but I was missing some of those "How tos" and social cues very early on.

I really didn't like the hardware I got stuck with—that was apparent early on. And that definitely contributed to getting really sad and depressed a lot. I'd been drawing pictures of myself as a girl all throughout the later years of elementary and middle school. Going into middle school, puberty age, 11 to 13 years old, I definitely knew I was not happy about things. I even had a teacher who figured things out and tried to get me in at a girls' conference once. I really wanted to go to it, but couldn't. I understood that boys couldn't go, but I didn't understand why *I* couldn't go, because I didn't identify as a boy at that point. Now it's structured that anybody that identifies as female can go.

At this point, I was no longer socially accepted by other boys, and the boys I did end up being friends with were either gay or genderqueer. From there on out, I was pretty much close with girls.

I started identifying as bi in middle school. I'm far more interested in women than men, but not exclusionary about that at all. I dated a great gay fellow in high school. A lot of my time at middle and elementary school was spent asking why things didn't work a certain way, and why we had such binary social categories, and why it had to be so segregated around gender lines. I bought a really beautiful turtle skirt on a field trip once, and being socially awkward, running around with a skirt and nail polish and combat boots was definitely eyebrow-raising. I just identified as me, not any of the available categories. Trans-female wasn't an option I was aware of at the time. Information was not accessible at that point; that could have done wonders.

I'd come out to partners and friends years before I came out to my parents. Because my parents are in the medical community, I would make an almost four-hour trip for my HRT treatments to make sure my parents didn't find out about it. I was on hormones for over half a year before coming out to family.

One winter after picking my brother up from the airport, I came out to him and then as soon as we got back to the house, we told my parents. My mom began connecting all the dots—it was like all the light bulbs got turned on at once for her. She was really happy and had concerns for my health and safety, but otherwise the world made a lot more sense to her. We were all hoping Dad didn't fall over with a heart attack, but his major freak out was over the fact that I was changing my last name, which I switched to my mother's last name. That part, I think, was harder for him up front. It's taken a couple of years for him to consistently get my name right. He's also struggled with using she/her pronouns. So that's been a harder toggle switch for him.

Medical Transition: There was definitely gatekeeping to get to my medical transition. I repeatedly ran into practitioners who were anti-trans. I also had ASD care cut off by anti-trans medical providers, who cancelled my prescriptions mid-transition, which was a really rough combination.

Estrogen has allowed me to flourish. Before surgery, I was on testosterone blockers (I don't need to take them now after surgery). Being at home in both my body and mind has been really good. To a certain degree, removing hardware that wasn't appropriate was more important than getting hardware that is appropriate. My bottom surgery is fine, but my top surgery isn't. They are larger than I wanted. It's not good for me, especially for my level of physical activity, and really not good for being in my head. I am working on fixing that.

Being ASD and Trans: Most people assume I'm *not* on the spectrum and chalk up missing certain social cues to poor social skills. For example, if I need to clear out of the room because the lights are flickering or something like that, some people who know me are like, "Oh cool, yeah, gotcha on that," but others don't understand why I can't hang out in certain spaces and why I have sensory overload shutdown mode. So, it's reminiscent of the comments that I used to get in school: "You're good at these things and therefore you should be good at all this other stuff. You're not trying hard enough." There's no real understanding of the asynchrony that happens with people for different things. These things about me are mostly invisible. Once folk in the queer community know that I'm also Aspie, that makes everything work a lot easier. But at first most people presume I'm not. So there's invisibility in many ways.

Being trans, you get a lot of assumptions across the board. People are curious, asking personal questions such as, "Do you like binary girls or boys, or did that switch all of a sudden?" It really helps hanging out with some of the queer-poly groups where people are more interested in individuals, rather than their specific hardware. I'm trans queer with a bi side; I'm mostly into women, though not ruling out anybody else.

I'm mostly into women but have a bi side. I'm trans tomcat queer, mostly into girls, but not ruling out anything else. I'm more reactive to the pheromones of the person. Sometimes, I get pushback from some more binary trans folk—predominantly trans women—who feel that the world should be more binary in certain ways and that I may be failing as a trans girl—for example, for not being able to speak in stereotypical female verbal patterns.

Personally, I think ASD and trans is a fabulous combination. I'm far less inclined to put other people in neat little nifty boxes. Some people are really fixated on pronouns and gender, whereas I've never really sorted people by these categories.

Romantic Relationships: I have a long-term significant partner that I'd known for over a decade prior to my transition. We've chased each other around continents, colleges, and through ups and downs. In the past, I wasn't aware how much they were really in love with me. At the time, nothing seemed right to me. I really loved being intimate with them, but sex was never what everyone described to me; it was never enjoyable and kind of a dysphoric mess for me. So much of this makes sense now.

When I started on HRT, we ended up spending a lot of time together and I began to actually read more of the social cues which helped me figure out just how much she liked me. We've worked through a lot of things. We are back to living in the same part of the world again and trying out poly. She's got another partner that she really likes. For us, poly makes the relationship stronger and intentional—to not have a restriction on it—that I'm stuck with them and not allowed to go on dates with people.

I've had some rough spots in all of my relationships around the autism spectrum stuff. I've really had to self-advocate at times and be like, "This is what I can do and what I can do easily and I'm perpetually going to miss some cues." Definitely putting it out there that people should be verbal about expressing themselves, and that I may not get some of the more subtle cues.

I think couples' counseling would be a fabulous thing now because of my awareness around the trans/Aspie stuff; those used to be the two white elephants in the room, as it were.

Poly Community: Poly is a really wonderful community of folk that I know down here, many of whom may or may not be dating anyone at this time but identify as poly. It's more about relationships than it is about romance in a sense. I've got friends that are poly and have a few different partners, but are asexual as far as sleeping with anybody. It's a really nice crossover on things.

Dating: I'm technically open to dating other people, but not currently in the market. I don't have the time or energy. Rather than vetting folks online, I would rather meet them through people I already know and who vouch for them. I didn't even bother trying to date when I didn't live within a social network. The return on effort just wasn't worth it. I didn't want to have to explain my life over a couple of dinners, be someone's token trans friend, their Aspie-weird friend, or their live-vicariously-through-experiences-in-my-life friend.

Advocating Partners: I may miss a lot of cues, so it really helps if partners are able to jump in and say what they think and what they feel. I prefer *advocating partners* or people who are a lot more verbally explicit in what they want. I encourage them to interrupt me and point things out if I'm not noticing something, and that's really big because otherwise I could be spending a ton of time asking, "What's up?" or "What are you thinking about? Is it related to me or not?" It helps to have frequent check-ins, conversations, and revisiting things like, "Let's check in next week about certain things," and making refinements.

My partner is good about making sure she has enough time for herself relevant to managing a poly relationship; however, she often overworks herself at her job. Both her other partner and I try to make sure that she is aware of her self-care time and needs. I do better with more frequent check-ins from people. I just need somebody to give me a call at lunch or at work and just make sure that I'm not in some dysfunctional loop cycle. I also need to ration my human interaction to make sure I get enough book and personal geek-out time.

Advice to Others: The Internet is your friend. Don't jump into any predefined boxes upfront. There's a significant amount of data that's out there that wasn't available in the past. There's also a lot of pressure to behave or conform to cishetero standards, but it's okay to be diverse, have differences in nuance. Keep researching. Keep learning. Your life is going to be better if you learn to continually adapt and learn, instead of putting up neatly defined categories. Do what you need to do to be safe and survive, but don't rush into predefined roles. Personally, I knew what I wanted physically at a very young age, but didn't know it was possible. I hated all the medical gatekeeper crap that was in my way. I had no clue what an amazing impact HRT was going to have on me, or I would've done it years earlier. I'm still here [alive], which is statistically improbable. But HRT at a younger age would have vastly improved that likelihood.

With regard to finding the right medical care, you don't want to go to a doctor who stopped learning or didn't change his mindset after school.

Don't stick with a shitty community either. Pick folks... You lose some people and you find some other people. They may or may not be in any matched category with you, but may happen to be nice awesome people that are great to have around on the planet and do things to help others.

Note: See Chapter 16 for an account from Alyia's partner, Catelyn.

Chapter 16

PARTNER PERSPECTIVE

Alyia's Partner: Catelyn

I think we both sometimes have to stop and try to figure out a "translation" when one of us is asking the other something they don't understand.

Name: Catelyn

Pronouns: She/Her

Age: 38

Education and Profession: Bachelors of Nursing; RN care manager

Living Situation: Alyia and I live separately. We are in a polyamorous relationship, and my other partner Sawyer (a somewhat femme/androgynous cis man), moved in with me earlier this year.

Diagnosis: Major depression. I sought counseling support after a couple of breakups due to ongoing feelings of depression and struggling to get back to a better sense of myself.

Gender Identity: I am a cis woman, insofar as I feel this is the best description of how I experience myself and identify in the world. I feel like my gender expression has shifted somewhat throughout my life, and I've often felt more aligned with a sense of self or roles that were androgynous (and occasionally male—for example, as a young child I wanted to grow up to be Luke Skywalker).

Sexual Orientation(s): I identify as queer, and have slowly come to take on the label bisexual as well, although the term "multisexual" as a link with others who experience attraction to multiple genders and/or body types feels more accurate (though it's not a widely used word). I've found my attractions have shifted over the years: I got to a point a few years ago where I was really only attracted to women and genderqueer people, and while that's still mostly true, I don't feel as exclusively that way now.

I don't know if it would work for Alyia and me to live together in the same house at this point. We've only lived together once, for a few months, and it wasn't all as good or healthy as I thought it would be at the time.

Ultimately what I see as an ideal living arrangement would be a small group of friends (maybe five or six of us in total) sharing a piece of land and living there in several separate houses, with Alyia and Sawyer being part of that. In the meantime, it's important to me that I can share with and make a kind of second home for Alyia.

Length of Relationship: We first got together in 2000. We've had a lot of off and ons since then. We had a long break up from 2009 to 2016, but we've slowly regained closeness since then. Last year we were able to talk about a lot of what happened between us in the past, and ultimately decided to be together again, with consent and agreement from my other partner.

Being Polyamorous: When Alyia and I were together in the past, it was pretty much always an open relationship, even when we weren't involved with other people. As Alyia put it back then, she didn't like "to define her relationships"—though sometimes, I would have preferred for us to be monogamous. I ultimately had polyamorous (poly) relationships with a few other people, but by my mid-30s, I'd decided that wasn't what I wanted for the long term. I kind of surprised myself when I realized I was willing to try being poly again. Alyia is actually more open to monogamy now—in some ways we've reversed how we feel about it. But even so, having more than one partner is not something I feel is an ideal for me in itself. I feel more like weird life circumstances have brought up this situation where there are two people: Alyia, from my past, and Sawyer, from my more recent life. I'd always felt drawn to Alyia prior to her physical changes, but now that she's finally bringing out more of her inner self, I feel even more of a connection to and love for her.

Family: I'd describe my family as white, lower middle-class, well educated. My mom's first thought when she met my dad was that he was "an anachronism." I grew up surrounded by big band jazz and cultural references from earlier times. I don't even think my folks had any music in the house from later than the 1960s, and they didn't get Internet service till well after I'd left for college, and as a kid I often felt kind of out of the loop culturally and socially around others my age.

My parents are pretty open and accepting, and I can tell them openly about my relationships and who my partners are. When they came to visit recently, all five of us hung out together. My mom tends to call autism (or pretty much any neurodiversity) "an affliction." I think she shows compassion, and a desire to understand, but she's more focused on the needs or difficulties it can cause for the person and those around them, than aware of the positive sides it could have. She and my dad are supportive of Alyia and our relationship. They struggle getting pronouns right, though they are putting in effort to get better at this.

My mom mentioned to me that she thinks both my dad and my brother have some autistic traits in their social behaviors—and I would add that they both have strong visual/spatial skills and intensive focus when engaged in projects of interest. My dad is a visual artist who builds intricate 3D dioramas, and my brother is an engineer who has always been fascinated with machines and building things.

Meeting Alyia: We met in college when we were 21, and quickly bonded over conversations about overseas travel and how this informed our perspectives of American culture. We both had a lot of critiques of mainstream culture and an appreciation of different ways of being, and this drew us to each other. I also remember we talked about being bi early on, and having that in common—though it was only years later that she told me about her gender and desire to transition physically.

In general, her intelligence and interest in social justice have always been turn-ons for me. When we were first getting to know each other, she told me about her experiences protesting. This ultimately led to me developing more political awareness and engagement in the years to come.

I appreciate how she's drawn to learn to do things really thoroughly and well (not just to a socially acceptable "good enough" level)—and uses her visual/spatial thinking abilities to always be on the lookout for the safety of others and her community. I've always felt and experienced her to be a very honest person, and someone who may get angry or mischievous, but is never ever manipulative or spiteful—she is someone who genuinely wants good outcomes for everyone.

She has a wonderfully wicked sense of humor and comes up with really original sayings and ways of describing things, which I love.

Coming Out: There's not much to say except that my own journey coming out has been quite different in that as a cis person I have not had to face having my gender questioned in a way that Alyia has.

Friendships and Social Life: Alyia is a lot more extroverted; she gets more energized by having people around doing lots of things, and readily plugs in to help with projects on a moment's notice. While I too value having connections with community, I do better having time to retreat. My other partner, Sawyer, is as introverted as I am and we often disappear to our respective parts of the house to do our own things separately.

As an introvert, I feel like it takes me longer to warm up to people and connect than it does Alyia. In the past, I always got my initial "in" into the communities there through her, and then over time developed my own circles tangential to the groups I connected with through Alyia.

As far as her ASD affects our social life—there are a few people in our circles of friends who don't get or are bothered by some of her ASD traits—like speech patterns and certain sensory reactions. Fortunately, most are reasonably good at interacting with and appreciating neurodiversity. On occasion, at social events, I feel like I have to choose between being present with her (such as when she is having a rough sensory-emotional time) and connecting with others. There are also a lot of wonderful people and things I've gotten to meet or be involved in because of her, and connections I might have missed without her and the ways her brain works, so I really appreciate that.

That said, it's not always clear to me what in our lives is related to her having ASD, what's due to my busy life and having another partner, and what's related to things she's gone through around gender transition (particularly with the stress, dysphoria, and depression she's experienced in the past year, which I know have made it harder for her to get out and be social).

Support System: Alyia's mom has been an important support for her, including accompanying her when she had her first surgery. And Sawyer, my other partner, has been incredibly supportive, not just of me taking time to spend with Alyia, but also in all three of us getting to hang out or going to events together, and making her always feel welcome at our house. We have several good friends who show up for us when we need help as well.

We also both have a goth/queer/local/weirdo/safe-space bar in town here where either of us can go and likely see somebody we know. The owner knows Alyia from years back and is a good friend of mine. It's the place that hosted a fundraiser party we held earlier this year for Alyia's surgery.

Together, Alyia and I have occasionally been involved with a local trans community group, and wish we had more time and energy to do more. We've both played D&D (Dungeons and Dragons) in different circles before and hopefully we can play together again at some point!

I've also periodically taken part in a friend's vaudeville storytelling troupe, and would love it if Alyia and I could both get to do this in the future. We also have circles we are involved with separately from each other that feed us—I'm part of a closed/esoteric spiritual group, and Alyia is connected with friends from a local Burner camp.

One community that has been particularly significant for both of us is a Radical Faerie home—primarily a sanctuary for gay men and trans folks, but it is very welcoming to a wide variety of genders. They hold big gatherings a couple times a year, and serve as a safe space year round for queer folks in need. Our experiences in the space created there for acceptance, exploration, celebration, and support for queerness have been profound for both of us.

ASD and Our Relationship: At age 21, I was vaguely aware of ASD as in I'd seen *Rain Man*, the movie. I had heard a little bit from my mom, a pediatric nurse, but was not aware of knowing anyone on the spectrum. I'm not sure when Alyia disclosed having ASD, but I think we'd known each other for a while by then. Of course it took me much longer to understand how ASD manifested in her behavior and our relationship.

ASD affects our relationship negatively and positively. In the earlier years of our relationship, I used to feel hurt by some of her behaviors. Now, I have come to understand that they may be part of her ASD—things like not saying affectionate goodbyes, fixating on World of Warcraft, cleaning her chainsaws for hours when I was trying to connect with her, or responding strangely when I tried to have a conversation with her about our relationship. Over time, I've come to understand that these were not attempts to be evasive, and had nothing to do with her feelings—or lack thereof for me. These things no longer bother me much (and she has changed a number of them too), but back then it was very difficult for me, and contributed in part to our long break up.

Besides ASD, she also has ADHD, and in the last year, she's been enduring a fairly intense depression. She often has a hard time using language when she has sensory/emotional meltdowns, and it can disrupt our plans, communication, or social interactions. I have to think fast to try to figure out what's affecting her during these times. I feel like I'm getting better at knowing how to respond.

On the positive side, she has a unique way of seeing things, and often picks up on things I don't. Hearing her thoughts is refreshing and inspiring, often adding a new perspective. She has amazing, detailed, inventive ideas—often hilarious, creative ways of commenting on or describing things. I sometimes find myself picking up some of her expressions or syntax, which feels good for my brain. She has strengths in her physical and spatial awareness, which seem to be related to ASD. She has a number of skills that I lack, which I very much appreciate. She helps me be spontaneous when she points out beautiful or interesting things (like a pattern of light, or swirling leaves), which I miss when busy or preoccupied. I like that we share some nerdy, intensive interests, such as geeking out about languages. Often there are times when we really get on the same wavelength, with things others might not understand—and it feels good without saying anything—we know we both appreciate it.

Awareness of ASD: It seems as though everyone I know now has at least some awareness of ASD. People associate it with social awkwardness and dislike for small talk, and sometimes they have an awareness of sensory overload. But a lot of people don't recognize the symptoms of someone experiencing sensory reaction or the ways someone with autism may need social/emotional support, but may be unable to express that. Working in the medical field, I realize many still associate autism with children rather than adults.

I'm not sure that ASD affects her understanding of gender and sexuality, but maybe it's helped her to think outside socially constructed boxes. ASD may affect her presentation and reaction to other people's expectations/conceptions of "female" behavior and appearance. The biggest impact I've seen is how sensory processing sensitivities affect her relationship with her body—things like what clothes and hairstyles she can be comfortable in. Her experience with surgery and anesthesia—and dealing with uncomfortable and significantly larger-than-desired breast implants. This has been really intolerable for her, given her constant and highly acute sensory and spatial awareness of her body.

The world/society we live in is not accommodating—and often hostile—to both trans and ASD folks, and this creates difficulties for Alyia. I get frustrated sometimes when I have difficulty understanding something she's experiencing or how she's expressing it. But I love how unique she is, how she's worked to understand how her brain works and the opportunities I've had to learn along with her. And I love how she's evolved in the years since we first met in embracing and expressing her gender.

Past Romantic Relationships: I think most of my partners have been either on the spectrum, or at least have had some autistic traits. One of my previous partners has a formal diagnosis of autism spectrum, and two others have said they strongly suspect that if they were evaluated, they would be diagnosed.

My partner, Sawyer, would probably not be given a diagnosis, but he loves D&D, *Star Trek,* immersing himself in learning, and honing a new skill. He reports that a previous partner asked him to show more facial expression to reveal more of how he was feeling.

My partners have had an interest in thinking independently and non-conventionally. They like to geek out and study and learn about complex things that interest them, and strongly value loyalty to a community and those close to them (all of which are important to me too). With a few of them, I sometimes felt there were less displays of affection towards me than I would have liked. Communication in these relationships was often full of welcome straightforwardness, mixed with feeling like it was sometimes difficult for me to get answers when I asked open-ended questions about our relationship.

Challenges of LGBTQ and Neurodiverse Relationships: I think there are societal challenges many other relationships don't have to contend with. In particular, there are all kinds of socioeconomic difficulties faced by both trans and autistic folks—of getting work to make ends meet, dealing with bureaucracies, and getting by in an often inhospitable social world. These things put stress on Alyia and thereby impact our relationship.

I also think there's more social pressure on trans women than cis women to act or present in stereotypically "female" ways in order to have their gender recognized or accepted. Being queer and autistic can challenge those stereotypes in various ways. And whereas queer identities and relationships are more widely accepted now than a couple decades ago, a number of people with ASD I've met have described running into people (often in the medical/mental health fields) who assume that someone with ASD doesn't really understand gender or can't have mature relationships.

In my relationship with Alyia, I definitely feel it's important for me to learn about and be aware of the things she has to deal with that I don't, and ways in which she may face discrimination or misunderstanding—both as a trans woman, and as someone with autism. That's a work in progress. There's a strength there too, in that we are pushed to understand things outside our comfort zones, be more flexible—and also to be more aware and empathetic to others different from us. We're also able to find humor in ways our relationship falls outside some social conceptions, like traditional butch/femme roles.

Making Accommodations for Each Other: When she gets into monologuing without checking in with me, I'm learning to take the initiative to interject with requests/reminders—which I would not feel comfortable regularly doing with someone else. She's super patient with me when I don't understand and get frustrated, or when I forget things that trigger her sensory-wise. And she encourages me to give her feedback about her social interactions and behaviors. She's also really good at being willing to explain—or assist me with—visual/spatial/mechanical things in our lives that I am oblivious about!

I think we both sometimes have to stop and try to figure out a "translation" when one of us is asking the other something they don't understand. We haven't been to couples counseling yet, but I think it could be helpful with a provider who is experienced with trans and autism spectrum clients.

Coping Strategies in Our Relationship: For me, this includes taking periodic alone time for myself to recharge, and getting support and connection with my other partner and friends. Sometimes I have to remind myself to let go of the nurse/caregiver mode and let Alyia take care of me, which she's often eager to do!

Having regular check-ins helps us—seeing how the other is doing day-to-day, and what each of us is expecting or desiring at a given time. I also try to keep learning about, and from, experiences of ASD folks and trans folks, both for general awareness and to help me gain insight and understanding about some things without needing explanations from Alyia.

I'd say that being in a poly relationship has changed a lot of my assumptions about how relationships are "supposed to be"—letting go of expectations, what communication needs to look like, and how I get support and my needs met. Being poly has its own challenges, such as how to make time for both partners and myself, while working full time, but there's a sense of flexibility and generosity in finding ways to make things work.

Having friends, and particularly my other partner, who show up for Alyia when needed and care about her has been hugely important. But I think the biggest thing is the long history of love and friendship Alyia I have had, the trust built over time, and the opportunity to figure out some of each other's patterns and inner workings over the years. For example, I know I'm a lot better now at not taking things personally, and Alyia is a lot better at expressing affection. And we both have the sense that our lives are deeply connected after all this time, that we're going to be there for each other no matter what.

Chapter 17

PARTNER PERSPECTIVE

Maya's Partner: Violet

Before Maya received the diagnosis—before we were even thinking about autism—we had a lot of difficulty communicating our needs to each other.

Name: Violet

Pronouns: She/Her

Age: 24

Education and Profession: Master's Candidate; pursuing a Master's in Social Work, specialization in Trauma and Interpersonal Violence

Living Situation: I live with my partner, Maya. We currently live together in a one-bedroom apartment.

Diagnosis: Hypersomnia, depression, and chronic pain

Gender Identity: Woman, cisgender

Sexual Orientation(s): Sometimes I use the word "queer," sometimes I use the word "lesbian." I deliberately prioritize women in all aspects of my life, especially in my relationships, whether they are romantic, platonic, familial, or sexual.

Length of Relationship: We have been together for about three and a half years.

Meeting Maya: I met Maya in college. We ran in similar circles and were involved in some of the same student groups, but we didn't begin being friends until our junior year. She was very cool, and I was always a little intimidated by her. Very smart, very stylish, very unapologetically gay in a way that was thrilling to me. Now I know that her quietness in groups is social anxiety, but at the time that vibe of bored aloofness made her seem way too cool for me. Our relationship was confusing for a while, in that weird space between close friend and girlfriend that can be so complicated amongst queer women, but it eventually grew into a strong partnership.

Coming Out: Coming out was more difficult for me than It was for Maya. The culture I grew up in is very different than the one Maya was raised in. Even when my mother leaned politically left of center, it was dangerous to be queer in that small, rural town. When I came out to her in high school, she had a difficult time with it, and for the sake of my relationship with her, I repressed it. It wasn't until late college that I was comfortable and confident enough with myself and my queerness that I was able to come out publicly, including my family and other people who knew me from home. Maya knew in elementary school that she liked girls, and as far as I know, nobody ever had any problems with that. Queerness in this country is still fraught with hurtful stereotypes and potential discrimination no matter where you live, but it was a much more accepting atmosphere for her.

Family and Past Relationships: I was raised by a single working mother in the rural West. Our community was made up of predominantly white, conservative, working-class folk. I was highly involved in the community through sports, arts, and community service. I also excelled academically, and my mother was very supportive of my education. There was a very strong culture, in both my family and the larger community, of "pulling yourself up by your bootstraps," and I worked very hard to achieve my goals.

My relationship with my mother was always very close, but has been tense since I began being more serious with Maya. Part of the tension is because we're two women, and part of it stems from my partner's quirks and my mother's limited view of how our dynamics differ from those of traditional, neurotypical couples. My mother knows that Maya is autistic and mentally ill, but she is still learning what that means. She's actually learning a lot just from observing my own relationship with Maya's mother, which is very close. She is making progress, but has a long ways to go toward understanding and unconditional acceptance.

The majority of my past relationships were with neurotypical men, and frankly, they're not worth mentioning. Maya is the first serious partner I've had since I really came out, and now that I know what it's like to be myself with a partner, none of my past relationships can hold a candle to this.

Before and After Maya's Autism Diagnosis: Before our relationship, I wasn't aware of ASD. I mean, I had heard *Rain Man* jokes and had a vague awareness that autism was a thing that existed, but I had never met anyone who was "out" of the autism closet until I got to college. And even at college, where I knew people who were autistic, it wasn't spoken about very often. It has only been in the past year or two that I've really come to a better understanding of autism, as both a diagnosis and an identity, and how it influences people in their daily lives.

Before Maya received the diagnosis—before we were even thinking about autism—we had a lot of difficulty communicating our needs to each other. We had no explanations or language for why or how we kept trying and trying and trying and failing to understand what the other person needed and how to give it. Now we know. Maya is autistic. I am not. Just that understanding alone has given us *so* many tools. We have resources, we have community, we have theory, we have coping strategies, we have a new appreciation for each other, we have patience for each other, we have a better understanding of each other. We know how to communicate what we need, we know what the other person is capable of giving, and we know how to manage when our needs are contradictory. Does Maya's autism negatively or positively affect our relationship? Neither. It just is. What do impact our relationship, usually negatively, are other people's perceptions and assumptions about our relationship when they learn about her autism. That can be hard on both of us, and we're still learning how to deal with it when it comes, but we have each other for support.

ASD and Our Relationship: At this point, it's hard to look at Maya and explicitly point out that "this, this, and this are autism." She just is who she is. She's autistic, so everything she does is autistic. Just like she's gay, so everything she does is gay. But I guess one of the traits that is pointed out to us most often by observers is her executive dysfunction, and what that means for me. There are a lot of things she can't do, or that she can do but are difficult/tiring/cognitively taxing, so I do them. It's mostly chores, housework, errands, things like that. The thing is, if I were in a straight relationship, it would be totally normal for me to take on the housework, and my male partner would be applauded for contributing his fair share. But since we're two women, people often comment that it's unfair or nonreciprocal. Maya and I don't think of reciprocity as "we each wash our own dish." Menial chores are so much easier for me to do. If we tried to split the chore list "evenly," I might feel fine and Maya would be completely out of energy for the day. *That's* nonreciprocal. We each give what we're able according to our individual capacities. That balance might look different for us than it does for non-ASD couples. We're proud of that.

Another trait is her echolalia, which, admittedly, is something I can point to and say "autism." Maya's echolalia has evolved into a shared language between us that has brought us closer just because of the sheer silliness of it. Many words, phrases, and sounds have entirely lost their original meaning and have been adopted into our lexicon. "Gyoza" means that it's time to wake up. "Ah-ah" can mean "I've arrived" or "that person is wearing a funny hat," depending on the tone and inflection. I can tell exactly how she's feeling based on a string of gibberish syllables, many of which have been turned into songs. Are non-ASD relationships this much fun?

Awareness of Autism: People aren't very informed about autism. A lot of harmful misconceptions abound, even from well-meaning but ignorant people. Some people respond with pity, others can't comprehend how an autistic person can have a relationship. Sometimes people speak to her like she's a child, or don't speak to her at all, and only interact with me. One of the most annoying reactions when I tell people my girlfriend is autistic is, "Oh, she must be high-functioning." What does that even mean? She's alive, that's functioning enough to be deserving of a loving and caring relationship.

Maya and her brother are both autistic. Her brother received his diagnosis at a young age. Maya did not receive one until she was 22, and only after she sought it out. There is a huge underdiagnosis of autism in girls, and one reason is because it can present so differently than it does in boys. In the last year, I think Maya has been really coming into an identity of what it means to be an autistic woman, not just a woman who is autistic. I wouldn't say that autism affects her understanding of her gender, but I do think it affects her experience of her gender.

Our Social Life as a Couple: While in college, Maya and I began our relationship after already being in the same friendship group, so we did share many of the same friends. We have both stayed in touch with some of those friends, but now that we're in different programs at different grad schools, our social lives are more separate. We do make an effort to get to know each other's friends, but for the most part, I think we both prefer to keep our own distinct social lives. We spend so much time together now that we live together, it's nice to have some time apart. All of my friends know that Maya is autistic—I've learned that if I don't say anything, Maya feels pressured to act "normal," or if she acts like herself (with occasional stimming, echolalia), sometimes new friends wonder if there's something wrong with her or feel unsure around her. Being open about her autism helps normalize her behaviors and make everyone more comfortable.

Support System for a Neurodiverse Couple: Maya's mother is our biggest source of support. She's wonderful. She is able to be supportive to both of us and help each of us meet our needs, even if those needs are conflicting. Of course she wants what is best for her daughter, but she also raised her and knows how stressful it can sometimes be when she and I are miscommunicating. She is a mother and a friend to us both.

Another support is one of Maya's friends from grad school. They have been friends long enough that I have been able to form a good relationship with her, and I have no hesitation reaching out to her if we need some extra help. Even if it's something as simple as giving her a heads up when Maya is having a bad day on her way to school, I know we can rely on her to cheer her up and help her with anything she might need that I can't give her.

LGBTQ and ASD Communities: We have made attempts to get involved with the queer community in Boston, but we sometimes have frustrations with the ableism and lack of accessibility in a lot of events and organizing geared toward queer folk. We'd love to be more involved with the disability community in Boston, but it can be tough to muster the energy for getting out and socializing. Between our classes, our internships, and all of our combined illnesses, we tend to be homebodies. Most of our communities are online. I'm in a Facebook group for people with similar sleep issues; she's a gamer, and is also on a listserv for people with psychiatric service dogs.

Couples Counseling: Our first couples counseling experience was a support group for neurodiverse couples facilitated by an ASD specialist. We had just made a lot of big changes in our lives—we had graduated college, moved to a new city, and were trying to navigate our separate lives while uncertain about the trajectory of our relationship. We were fighting all the time, with huge screaming matches that left both of us exhausted and sad and hurt. Maya was in the process of receiving her diagnosis when we started going to the group. The group was awesome. We realized pretty quickly that, even though we were so much different than the other couples (much younger, unmarried, and gay), we found more in common with them and were more comfortable with them than we were in most 20-something-oriented queer spaces. Eventually, Maya's class schedule conflicted with the group, and we had to stop going. We started couples counseling with the group facilitator, and it was illuminating in many ways, but we ended when we realized that what we really needed was individual counseling for our own issues.

Accommodations We Make for Each Other: There are small things and it is hard to even remember that they are accommodations and not just what everyone does. Like, making sure to turn on the lamp instead of the overhead light in our living room, because her eyes are sensitive; or making sure the TV or music system is at the correct volume before I turn it on, so it's not too loud; or anticipating any and all potential loud sounds so I can give a heads-up so she doesn't startle—anything from the mixer if I'm baking to the doorbell if someone is coming. Eating strong-smelling food (especially peanut-butter or cheese) in a different room so it doesn't bother her. Deferring to her on all interior decorating or major purchases, because she is very particular and I like it when she's happy.

Maya works very hard to accommodate any needs that I have. Even though she likes being hugged, she really does not like being the hugger, but she'll still wrap an arm around me or pat my shoulder when I'm feeling down. She never makes me feel guilty about going to sleep early when I'm very tired, even though we both know that she has difficulty motivating herself to go to bed when she's alone at night. She's always aware when I'm in pain, and takes good care of me by making sure I take my meds and insisting that I rest—a task that is usually a test of wills which she inevitably wins. I'm sure she does other things that I don't even recognize as accommodations because they're so ingrained in our daily interactions.

Strategies We Use as a Couple: Communication. Communication. Communication. If we could only choose one coping strategy to live with, we could be happy forever with just communication. It's such a stereotype of lesbians, but we talk about *everything*. If we're working or playing in the same room together, we check in periodically to see if the other needs to switch their activity or if they need anything. If we disagree on what to have for dinner, we then talk about how we handled the disagreement. If we are doing *anything* that will interfere with the normal routine of the day, we give each other a heads-up. If either of us is having a good day, we process it. If either of us is having a bad day, we process it. If one of us misinterprets anything the other has said or done, we go on and on about what we said and what we meant and what we're feeling and what every barely distinguishable facial expression could mean. I mean, seriously. We talk a *lot*. It's awesome. And it's not all verbal! When Maya gets very agitated and goes nonverbal, we have text-to-speech apps and a portable whiteboard and some basic Sign/American Sign Language (ASL) to get us through.

We Don't Let Others Dictate How We're Supposed to Be Together: I kind of alluded to this before, but I think the biggest challenge we face being both queer and neurodiverse is finding a social group where we fit. Between ableism in the queer community and heteronormativity in the autism/neurodivergent community, it's difficult to feel understood or appreciated. And the overlap in the Venn diagram of those communities is so, so small.

And, of course, society beyond our marginalized groups isn't sure what to do with us. I think it's difficult for people to reconcile the fetishization of lesbian couples with the infantilization of autistic people and the stereotype of women as "natural caregivers." People don't/can't understand that this girl having a meltdown at a crowded train station is the same girl who will crawl into bed with me and kiss me goodnight; that *all* relationships have nuance, and that our relationship doesn't have to fall into a preconceived box of what relationships between women—intimate, caregiving, friendly, whatever—are "supposed" to look like. Our biggest strength is that we know that, and we make our relationship look like whatever we want it to, whenever we want, however we want, and we don't let others dictate how we're supposed to be together.

Being with My Autistic Partner: Oh this is going to sound so cheesy. I'm so in love with Maya. That's it, that's the big secret to our successful neurodiverse relationship. She just is who she is, and I love every part of her. Being together has been far from easy, but it has been simple, because at the end of the day, she makes me be my best version of myself, and I want to do whatever she needs to help her be and do whatever she wants, because I love her.

Chapter 18

PARENT PERSPECTIVE

Jo Jo's Father: Fred

My wife or I both responded with a statement similar to "It doesn't matter who you are attracted to or what their gender or color is, as long as they are good to you and you feel supported. What matters is that you are treated with love and respect."

Name: Fred

Pronouns: He/His

Age: 63

Education and Profession: Master's in Business Administration; contracts manager

Living Situation: I am divorced, and as part of that process have had to sell my home. So, I am living single at an apartment.

Diagnosis: I have never been diagnosed or evaluated for anything.

Gender Identity: Cisgender man

Sexual Orientation(s): Straight

Raising Jo Jo: Both of my children are queer. My younger child, Jo Jo, is high-functioning autistic and agender. Jackie, who's older, self-identifies as having emotional challenges but has not been diagnosed; she is married to a same-sex partner and holds a successful job.

The social aspect of school was always difficult for both of our children. We did playdates and encouraged both kids to meet with friends; however, neither of our children seemed to have a lot of friends. That being said, making friends seems to be one of those things that is easier for some children than for others.

We maintained an environment in the home of acceptance and openness. Our local religious center also provided an excellent educational program on sexuality called "Our Whole Lives." I am certain that this environment and education made it easier for both children to feel that they could express their queer identities when they came out. Even today, Jo Jo lets me know how glad they were, and how unique it was, that we provided such a loving and accepting environment for them.

Current Family Relationships: My wife and I are currently going through a divorce. We've had some rough times during the marriage, which we know had a negative effect on the children.

Jo Jo was living at home at the time my wife and I separated, so my relationship with them has grown very close since my wife left. I feel that the absence of my wife allowed Jo Jo and me to live closer to our true selves.

Jo Jo has developed a lot in the past year and is now living with their significant other in another state across the country. They are also preparing to go to college this fall to study psychology.

It seems that Jackie relates better to her mother, and Jo Jo to me. Overall, we all get along pretty well, although there are strained moments from time to time.

Jo Jo's Diagnosis: Jo Jo had a psychiatric evaluation confirming autism when they were 18 years old.

In retrospect, when Jo Jo was around three or four years of age, I noticed Jo Jo getting involved in very intensely focused activities. They would sit for long periods of time and focus on "reading" (looking at books), or buckling and unbuckling their shoes until they could do it well. As I was not aware of how autism manifests, these events just appeared to me to be related to advanced childhood development.

When Jo Jo first started school, they were put into first grade early as a result of testing but was later transferred to kindergarten due to an inability to make transitions between work, as well as difficulty with legible handwriting. It was clear that Jo Jo was very intelligent, but had some other areas that seemed to not fit with the school system's formula for development.

It wasn't until 5th grade that a teacher suggested we have Jo Jo formally evaluated. At that time the diagnosis they received was ADHD and the evaluator suggested that we consider applying to get Jo Jo into a different, more supportive school. In retrospect, this was the best decision we made and probably saved Jo Jo's life.

Also around the age of six or seven, Jo Jo became less affectionate. Jackie continued to enjoy hugs and sitting on laps for story time; however, Jo Jo seemed to be more solitary and seemed to be more cerebral rather than physical.

Their interest in Math and Science developed rapidly throughout school. For the most part, it was good to know that Jo Jo was advanced in many ways. In short, a gifted child. But, we did not associate this with autism. We often spoke about Jo Jo as being the absent-minded professor—so brilliant in some ways and so forgetful in other ways. These were more autistic characteristics but with no knowledge of autism, I never would have made the connection.

Jo Jo was admitted to a children's psychiatric facility at age 17 after disclosing that they had depression and suicidal ideation. This is when they were finally identified as having autism.

As an "invisible disability," autism—and any mental illness—can easily go undetected, and as parents the diagnosis was critical in triggering us to pay more attention to the support that Jo Jo needed. The first ADHD diagnosis prompted us to change schools. The second diagnosis reaffirmed the need for extra support and applying for financial disability support from the state.

My wife had suspected autism early on, but no one concurred with her observations at the time.

It was a relief to Jo Jo, after they accepted the diagnosis (which was accomplished only after researching many Internet memes about autism—the modern way for children to seek new information), they were relieved that they were not certifiably crazy.

In particular, Jo Jo has synesthesia, which is where their senses get jumbled. Prior to the diagnosis, this caused them to realize they were different from others, but they did not realize this was a known condition related to autism.

In a related story, after the diagnosis, Jo Jo and I were browsing in a bookstore and I saw a workbook on PTSD. Jo Jo dove into the book and realized that they matched the diagnosis for complex PTSD

100%. They did discuss this with their therapist and worked on this in treatment.

Coming Out: Jo Jo began to act more like a tomboy around age seven. At age 14 they held a "family meeting." When Jo Jo called the family meeting, we were concerned as it seemed like it might be a topic of significant concern. As it turned out, Jo Jo informed us that they were bisexual. We breathed a sigh of relief as this was not an issue at all. My wife or I both responded with a statement similar to "It doesn't matter who you are attracted to or what their gender or color is, as long as they are good to you and you feel supported. What matters is that you are treated with love and respect."

Around 18 they were talking more about being genderqueer and non-binary. Shortly after, they continued to describe variations in gender identity.

ASD and LGBTQ: After finding out about both Jo Jo's ASD and LGBTQ status, we simply continued to support and accept them as we always had. The autism diagnosis of course created a need for greater involvement to obtain assistance. We also felt the need to become more educated and to become advocates for a more accepting community around gender issues.

Most people do not seem very aware of ASD. They don't understand the reality, having based their knowledge on popular media such as the *Rain Man* movie; or their reference point for autism is based on someone with severe and obvious problems they may have encountered. Few people, even within my own family, have an understanding of the invisible disability of a high-functioning autistic. I didn't know much about it myself prior to my experience with Jo Jo.

I find that older people, including myself, were brought up with two options: a person was either gay or straight. Not to mention certain groups whose beliefs would deny or disallow such expressions. Today, most young people seem to be familiar with gender variability.

There are many movies, documentaries and magazine articles around the subject of gender identity, which adds credibility to the individuals who are experiencing gender variability. Hopefully, people will understand that gender is more than a simple "decision" on their part.

How Having a Queer Child Has Changed Me: Mainly Jo Jo's and Jackie's journeys has prompted more self-reflection, and made me open to possibly shaping these identities for myself. It also reaffirmed my own self-image as an open and accepting parent. But, it also highlighted how easy it is for a parent to be blind to the experiences of their children, and to young people in general, when one spends most of one's time in a heteronormative and non-ASD adult world.

Acceptance within the Extended Family: All family members, my wife's and mine included, have been accepting and kind, even if they don't have a full understanding of the gender environment or autism. For example, when we explained that Jo Jo can become overwhelmed at family gatherings and may have to leave abruptly, they accepted this and continued to be welcoming to our family at all family events.

Advice to Other Parents: Read as much as you can both on gender and autism. Educate yourself as much as possible from both external sources and from listening to your child. Join autism advocacy organizations. Be aware of what is going on in your child's education system and seek alternatives if the system is not working. A bad school environment can exacerbate the issues and cause more harm down the road.

Get a good therapist that specializes in these issues and make sure your child is connecting well with that therapist. We were fortunate to find a therapist who understood autism and gender identities and could make a solid connection with Jo Jo.

Maintain love, kindness, and acceptance in a non-judgmental way (unconditional positive regard). Understanding and acceptance are different and you need both. Accept your children for wherever they are and whoever they are.

Chapter 19

PARENT PERSPECTIVE

Xiomara's Mother: Myra

It is difficult to see beyond one's own world and perspective. But although I'm straight and neurotypical, I love my daughter and I love her personality.

Name: Myra

Pronouns: She/Her

Age: 58

Education and Profession: College; financial advisor

Living Situation: Xiomara left home four years ago to go live with her girlfriend, so I live alone with the beautiful company of our dog, Ganesh.

Diagnosis: I don't have any mental health diagnosis, I sometimes joke about being a little OCD, but it's nothing serious because it has never been an issue for me at all and I have never looked for a diagnosis, so I guess the answer is no.

Gender Identity: Cisgender woman

Sexual Orientation(s): Straight

My Understanding: My understanding of gender identity is that it is how you identify yourself: you can identify yourself as male or female and sometimes that doesn't match your body. Sexual orientation is the attraction you feel towards others: it can be towards someone from the opposite sex and sometimes someone of your own sex or it could be both.

As for the Asperger's/autism, Xiomara is my only child, so I never compared her to anyone else. She was so calm and shy, but I always believed it was just her personality because her dad was just like that. It never occurred to me that she was in the spectrum at all; I just thought she was different. She was really intelligent and focused in subjects and topics that were not seen as "normal," but for me this was not strange, I thought she just had different interests and being social was not one of them.

Since a very early age, my daughter was more interested in sports and other things and not interested in boys. At the time I just thought she was still young and that she would show those interests later on, but I guess that once she was a teenager I started thinking she might be gay. At first it was difficult, and I didn't have the courage to ask her directly.

Xiomara's Coming Out: Xio told me she wanted to talk to me about something. She was 21. We sat down together and I let her talk. She talked to me about her relationship. It was her first relationship, with a woman 14 years older than her—this was the shocking part, and that is what I told her. I told her I already knew she was gay, that I had figured it out, but that I was waiting for her to be ready to tell me.

Xiomara's Asperger's/Autism: I think in general people have this black or white perspective about autism. Not many people are aware of all the shades or all the possibilities within the spectrum. In our society, at least here in Mexico, people are not educated in terms of ASD, which is very sad because many kids and adults are not being diagnosed, they are being bullied and treated as "different." The world needs to understand that being different is what makes the world amazing and rich.

One day, Xio told me that when she read some aspects about Asperger's she felt related to that. She told me that she would try to contact someone who might help her understand more about it and discover if she had it, which would explain many things. I encouraged her to do it. The diagnosis of Asperger's was eye-opening, because I also discovered that my husband had it too and we didn't know. Xiomara's diagnosis was not a surprise; it was just exciting to know that this type of wonderful personality has a name.

Xio receiving the Asperger's diagnosis didn't change a lot for us, but we now know what it is and we learn more about the topic everyday. Xio didn't have many challenges to begin with due to her Asperger's traits. I guess the only thing I could say is that I am more aware of her difficulties and more understanding about them.

LGBTQ Awareness: The problem is not a lack of information, because I think these topics are becoming more popular and common; however, this doesn't mean they are accepted. There is still a lot of discrimination. At least now the LGBTQ community has more presence and it's a community that is becoming stronger and they are having more confidence in themselves as a group, but it's still taboo. These things are still something uncomfortable for many people.

Asperger's and Gay: My daughter told me, "Hey, so this means I'm an Aspergay." She was excited about that. I guess people are not really aware of this, I don't think they even consider that there might be some people that are both gay and autistic. My daughter sees it differently: she thinks it was easier for her to accept her Asperger's diagnosis because she had already accepted she was different and she was part of a minority, so now she says she is part of two minorities.

Acceptance: It is difficult to see beyond one's own world and perspective. But although I'm straight and neurotypical, I love my daughter and I love her personality. I raised her to be a good person, with good values. Most importantly, I raised her to be happy and to live her life in the best possible way and I think I have succeeded in that.

Being the parent of a child who identifies as LGBTQ and autistic has taught me to see all the shades, all the possibilities and perspectives in life. And to be more understanding and respectful.

Unfortunately we have some members in our family who wouldn't accept the fact that she is gay, and I have told my daughter that I will defend her no matter what, but it has been her choice not to tell them yet. I have shared this with friends (both the Asperger's diagnosis and the fact that she is gay). The people that know these things have known her for many years so they support her.

My Relationship with Xiomara: I myself had a good childhood, but my mother wasn't at home most of the time because she was always working. Although I have always worked, I was also very present and involved in my daughter's life. Xio is an only child, so we have a very close relationship and a very good one. We have a lot of fun, and although we are very different, we share so many things in common and we understand each other and respect each other. Bringing up kids is never easy, but what is important is educating them and teaching them to be patient, to be caring and respectful, and showing them all the values that are important in life.

We are a very small family. My closest relationship is with my Xio. Although she no longer lives with me, she lives two blocks away, so we get to spend a lot of time together. I look after my mother and aunt—they live close to my home as well, so we are always in touch and looking after each other.

Advice to Other Parents: I would tell them to be respectful, patient, and to put themselves in their child's shoes so they can see things differently and from their perspective. I would tell them that coming out as gay, transgender, receiving an ASD diagnosis, or any other thing that makes you different is very difficult. Our kids are very brave! We should support them and be proud of them.

Part 3

DISCUSSION

ASD AND LGBTQ IDENTITIES

Common Themes Across the Narratives

Once we completed the interviews and reviewed the stories of our participants, we were struck by the common themes across these individual narratives and stories. Although each person has their own unique constellation of intersecting identities, there are global ways in which they experience their intersecting autistic and LGBTQ identities. For this book, we wanted to ensure that each individual had the opportunity to share their story in their own words, but also found it important to highlight overlapping themes for readers so that they may consider how these personal examples may apply to their own lives. To better understand these stories as a whole, the concept of thematic analysis was used, which is a flexible methodology in which patterns are identified, analyzed and reported (Braun and Clarke, 2006). Below are the overarching themes in the stories, along with quotes that best highlight them, as well as a discussion on the implications and conclusions of these findings.

Theme One: Awareness of Sexual Orientation and/or Gender Identity from an Early Age

There is a misconception that autistic people are not able to identify their sexual orientation or gender identity (Gougeon, 2010). In a recent qualitative study on individuals who are transgender and autistic, some participants noted that providers used autism as a way of invalidating their gender identity (Maroney and Horne, 2018). Participants in this study largely spoke of an awareness of their sexual or gender minority identities from a young age. For instance, **Alyia** reflected on gender identity: "A lot of middle and elementary school was me asking why things didn't work a certain way, and why we had such binary social categories, and why it had to be so segregated around gender lines." While **Olivia** shared: "I wrote in my diary that I was bi at the age of ten, soon after learning the word." This was reported by most participants, but not all, as reflected by **Annie**, who stated about her sexual orientation: "I wish it hadn't taken me until I was 30 to figure it out, but it did."

For some participants, language or labeling their identity was a big part of this awareness and acceptance of their identity. For those who are able to find labels to describe their experience and sense of self, it is often very empowering. **Taylor** was one individual who reported this:

> As soon as I learned about non-binary genders (genders existing outside of the binary of male and female), I felt like part of me that had been repressed could finally express itself, and have a name. It took me a few months to settle on the identity that felt the closest to what I was, since I had been trying to ignore that part of myself for most of my life.

As highlighted by **Jo Jo**, some individuals may struggle until finding the correct language, or may feel alone in this: "I always knew I wasn't a girl, but I figured I must be, because I knew I wasn't a boy either." It is important to clarify that this early self-awareness did not necessarily mean participants came out to others at this age. This awareness often signaled an outness to oneself with identity, but autistic LGBTQ individuals—much like we often hear from non-spectrum (NS) LGBTQ individuals—may worry about rejection or discrimination, or simply may not be aware that identities can exist outside of the conventional norms. For instance, the dominant discourse of gender as binary, with the options being male or female, or heterosexuality as the expectation for sexual orientation, can be very restrictive, and may delay self-acceptance of gender identity or sexual orientation(s): "I first had inklings that I wasn't a girl when I was six, but I repressed it for years" (**Cliff**).

Theme Two: Coming Out Is a "Gradual" and "Lifelong" Process That Differs with Context and Identity

When many think about coming out, it is usually as a single event in which someone "comes out of the closet" with their sexual orientation. Outness is much more complex, often made up by many moments in which an individual may choose to reveal or not share their identity, depending on their sense of safety and trust. As highlighted above, participants often came out to themselves at a younger age, but many reported coming out to others later, and a number of times to the people in their life. As stated by **Alyia**, this awareness even has been a "gradually over time thing," with her "realizing there was a disconnect on a few different levels." Experiences of coming out can differ based on to whom, when, how, where, and many other factors. As eloquently stated by **Gannon**: "At times when I did come out, it was stressful, shameful, liberating."

Participants varied in their decisions to come out with sexual orientation to friends or family, with some reporting early supportive familial experiences, while others noted that friends were the people they first wished to share this with. As shared by **Nijah**: "I told my mother I liked everyone when I was 13. She didn't even mind it. My mother was the first person to be accepting of it, so I didn't feel a need to tell others." The decision to come out, and continuously come out, is very personal, and may vary with the individual. For **Annie**, who realized her sexual orientation later in life: "Once I figured out I was gay I told everyone. It was a 'yahoo!' kind of thing." The response from others can be very impactful, as highlighted by **Cliff**, who noted coming out as bisexual in high school was "weird, lots of awkward fetishizing by classmates." **Sam**, who came out at 28, experienced reactions to her autism when sharing her lesbian identity: "Some people around me concluded, 'Aha, that's why she is odd,' but I think actually my 'oddness' is due to the ASD."

The decision to come out with a gender identity other than cisgender (e.g. transgender) is often a different experience than that of coming out about sexual orientation. Transgender individuals face high likelihood of experiencing rejection, discrimination, and violence as a result of their identity. For **Taylor**, friends were the community they felt comfortable sharing with: "They asked a few questions to try and understand it better, and have been very supportive and respectful. They recognize that although my pronouns are different now, I'm still me." Coming out as transgender can clash with family beliefs, making it important to create a "family of choice" or a community which is supportive of identities. This was the case for **Phoenix**, who comes from a culturally Hispanic family and faced invalidation from their family:

> My parents don't acknowledge any of my identities, wishing to view me as a "normal cis adult" so I don't bring shame on them or our family. I have a better relationship with my siblings, but they also don't acknowledge me, refusing to use my preferred pronouns.

Many spoke about their experiences coming out as autistic, which may be less well known outside of autistic communities. Those coming out as autistic risk ableist comments and judgment. The experiences of the participants varied in terms of finding acceptance. Some noted their "passing privilege," or the ability to be viewed as NS due to camouflaging autistic traits or working to improve social skills. For **Yaeli**, coming out as autistic has meant that she's often questioned by others because of their preconceived notions of what it means to be autistic:

> When I do come out about ASD, I definitely feel like people must have some image in their head of someone who is less capable. So they are always saying things like, "Oh you couldn't have it!" So I feel like in that sense people may not have the impressions that I would like them to have.

For some, coming out as autistic can negatively impact the view others have of them, particularly related to ability. As shared by **Nijah**, coming out to her boss due to challenges in her job has raised new fears: "Now, I think that because they know I'm autistic and have proof, they may try to get rid of me."

Theme Three: Finding Community, Often with Those Who Share Identities, Is Affirming to Me

Participants spoke about the importance of finding a community where they could be themselves and feel accepted. They reported feeling "less alone" when they found others who understood their experience and identities, and "unconditionally accepted" them. **Mario** reported: "Finding acceptance and understanding in my partner and friends, who are in many ways my family of choice, has been most affirming to me." In many cases, their found/adopted community was a space where others shared one or more identities with them, and in some cases interests or hobbies, such as kink, gaming, anime, or cosplay. Shared identities were reported to be a "strong connector." As stated by **Phoenix**:

> Birds of a feather flock together... Many of my friends also have non-conforming identities. It has brought my friends closer to me, we share something in common. It also helped bring trust and bonds. They know that I love them as they are and will not deny them of their identity.

For many, their communities also validated their own gender identity or sexual orientation and assured them that their identity was not, as **Taylor** put it, a "'crazy notion' [they] made up." These communities, also gave some a "safe space" to explore aspects of their identity they may not have otherwise. For instance, **Yaeli** spoke about the importance of joining a Harry Potter fandom as a way to "figure out [her] transness" by "trying out genders" that fit her experience in a safe space. This sentiment was also shared by **Annie**:

> Once I found myself around lesbians, I immediately felt happier and more accepted. My life became much better in numerous ways. With such a broad spectrum of masculinity and femininity, I fit right in. I also discovered I only glam out and wear makeup, jewelry, etc. when I am to be around lesbians. I feel quite uncomfortable in this attire in the straight world. It's a piece of gender identity that only occurs in a limited context, but that makes it fun.

The intersection of ASD-LGBTQ identities often presented difficulties within the general LGBTQ Community and sometimes even in autistic communities. For instance, they found aspects of the "stereotypical gay community," such as the hookup culture and bar culture, "strange" and not always conducive to the sensory needs of those on the spectrum. There were limited spaces where folks felt comfortable meeting others, as well as issues with feeling uncomfortable meeting new people or being in new situations.

> **Olivia**: Being autistic and bi and pansexual makes it much more easier to understand intersectionality, but also makes it harder to fit into the larger LGBTQ community. I don't really like bars, loud noises, or

> crowds (e.g.. Pride), which are like pretty big areas for LGBTQ people to meet other LGBTQ people.

Although people sometimes shared one identity with a particular group or community which they assumed would be accepting, they still felt othered or faced invalidation for their intersecting identities.

> **Taylor**: Even in groups for ASD and LGBTQ communities, I sometimes feel like I do not belong. Within LGBTQ spaces, my asexuality and non-binary identities are occasionally scoffed at—sometimes they are not taken seriously if individuals know I am autistic. It is hard to find places where I feel safe and accepted, even in alleged "safe spaces."

Theme Four: Being ASD-LGBTQ Is a "Fabulous Combo" but "Living in a Neurotypical, Cisnormative, and Heteronormative World Often Makes Me Feel Like I'm Not Quite Human"

While narrating their stories, participants reflected on the ways they benefited from their intersecting ASD-LGBTQ identities, while also noting challenges with how they were conceptualized or seen by others. For instance, several people noted that their identities made them more open-minded, better able to "step outside myself" and "less likely to put people in neat nifty little boxes," which helped them to understand others with different or non-normative identities. They also generally spoke positively about being outside of the normal/stereotypical boundaries of society.

> **Xiomara**: I'm sure many people would consider being gay and Asperger at the same time some sort of tragedy—like you have two things that make you less normal—but I see it the other way around. I just think that these two aspects of myself are just part of my personality and I don't see myself being or wanting to be different at all. I like the things that make me me.

The participants highlighted their difficulties related to holding multiple marginalized identities, which often opened them up to discrimination or invalidation of their identities. Despite these pervasive challenges, participants in this book showed great resilience, and prioritized their sense of self in the face of these challenges. **Maya** reflected this balance:

> Being a woman is hard, and an autistic woman more so, and maybe a queer autistic woman even more. At some point, one is so far from normative society that it stops mattering and I am less able to pull these various elements of myself apart when I think of who I am overall.

There exist a number of misconceptions about autism, and even more so about the intersection of being autistic and LGBTQ. For instance, individuals reported that people around them often expressed that "autistic people can't be gay because they have to be all asexual." They viewed autism and sexual orientation as "separate categories," or believed that "autistic [people] shouldn't be able to come out or self-identity as anything but cis and hetero because those things are seen as default settings" (**Cliff**). These biases were often evident in their interactions with others, when they came out with an identity, and were met with rejection as highlighted by **Taylor**: "I have seen people try to discredit [autistic] individuals saying that they have something 'broken' in their brain...which has resulted in their LGBTQ identity." In some cases, based on the stereotypes others had internalized, our participants were told by them that they couldn't possibly be autistic or LGBTQ, even when they were directly disclosing their identities with them.

> **Sam**: Usually people would "assure" me that I wasn't on the autism spectrum as if it was a bad thing. They assumed because I was female, I couldn't be. And also, if I can make eye-contact and have a firm handshake (self-taught behavior using business books) then I cannot be on the spectrum. Strangely, I had a similar experience when I expressed attraction to the same sex. It was assured that I couldn't be gay because I can wear a dress (when need be) and was feminine (enough). There is also a "hush-hush-I-won't-tell" attitude that I find strange. Like there is something to be ashamed of. Being in the minority does not equal bad.

Theme Five: Employers Have No Idea How to Respect and Bring Out the Best of Autistic Employees

Our participants reported both challenges and benefits in the workplace as a result of their intersecting identities. Some of them viewed their autism as a strength, and also saw their traits which are commonly associated with autism (see the Appendix) as an asset to their career or current job. Throughout these stories, folks shared their feelings that being autistic led to some work opportunities, such as attending MIT, becoming an engineer, a line cook, and working in IT Security. For instance, **Gannon** noted that "the combination of ADHD and autism, sort of nit-picky, high energy, wanting to keep track of multiple things all at once, while also being precise in how to pull these things off, doing more things than you possibly can" has actually helped him thrive at his job. This sentiment was echoed by **Mario**, as shown below:

> I credit my Asperger's with some of my tendencies towards logical thought and systems-oriented thinking. This helps with my IT security career quite a bit, as I can often troubleshoot or figure out problems and see consequences faster than many others.

Participants also reflected on the difficult process of finding careers or jobs that aligned well with their autistic identity. For **Annie**, "It took a long time to gain the understanding that I have zero interest in jobs that are excessively 'people-y,'" which ultimately led to her current job that she feels is a good fit for her. **Jo Jo** shared the experience of losing two jobs because of social difficulties. Due to the prevailing lack of understanding of autism and how to best support autistic employees, several individuals shared that they worried about the disclosure of their autism to their employers or coworkers, and were concerned about how they may be perceived. "I also struggle with imposter syndrome, not feeling enough—educated enough, expert enough" (**Cliff**).

Coming out as LGBTQ in the workplace or for prospective jobs was also identified as a source of high anxiety and fear. **Taylor** remarked: "Unfortunately my current workspace is not the safest place to be out about my gender. I am afraid to apply to other jobs since I worry I might find it to be similar to my current job, or even hostile to my identities." Individuals worried about discrimination and hostility, and one person lost a job for presenting as gender non-conforming (see **Silas**'s story). Others reflected on the ways their identities may have privileged them in their careers, as compared to others with shared identities. As shared by **Annie**, "As a lesbian, I wince at how much more I make than any of my friends," while **Yaeli** reflected, "I'm sure that I've been very lucky as someone who is white and for a long time was viewed as male."

Reflections

In considering these themes that have emerged from the stories/narratives in our book, it is important to consider the context of who our participants are, and also reflect on whose narratives we might be missing. The majority of participants are from the Northeast in the U.S.A., either living there now or having lived there in the past, with several exceptions, as two grew up outside of the U.S.A. This is a result of the authors' location, and should be considered when reading these narratives. A majority of the participants are white and middle to upper-middle class. We believe that the narratives that are missing are those from ethnic minorities, as well as those from the lower socioeconomic sections of society.

The adults who shared their stories are living fulfilled lives, with supportive families, friends, and partners if they choose to be in relationships. At the time of the interviews, the majority of participants were in a relatively good place, despite past challenges. Unfortunately this is not the dominant narrative when we consider the stereotypes about autism and ability in general. It is important to restate that the majority of these individuals became connected with us as a result of seeking therapeutic services, whether it be individual, group, or couples therapy. Finally, it is important to reflect on who would volunteer to participate in a project like this, and the timing of when someone might choose to share their story. Clearly, those who chose to participate in our book were in a stable enough place in terms of family, friends, community, education, employment, and even relationships (for some).

Many of the challenges highlighted above, such as outness, finding communities of support, and navigating experiences of discrimination vary by geographic location. Although we shared the stories of a couple individuals who grew up outside of the U.S.A., it is important to mention the global context. The ways that LGBTQ individuals are viewed across the world varies dramatically by region or country, making outness or finding others with shared identities a risky endeavor (Human Rights Watch, 2018). For example, in some places it is against the law to come out as gay. In addition, the ways autistic individuals are viewed also varies by country. Although many of the themes we've outlined may apply to many people globally with these intersecting identities, it is important not to overlook who the individual is, where they're living, who they have in their lives, and other intersecting identities like race or religion.

ACCEPTANCE, UNDERSTANDING, AND HOW TO HELP—FOR FAMILY, FRIENDS, AND COUNSELORS SUPPORTING ASD-LGBTQ INDIVIDUALS

Q and A with Eva and Meredith

1. Is there a higher than average overlap between ASD and LGBTQ?

Eva: Yes, there seems to be. Researchers have been discovering that there is an overrepresentation of gender variation in individuals with ASD vs. the general population (George and Stokes, 2016; Janssen, Huang and Duncan, 2016). In addition to gender diversity, ASD individuals also had higher rates of asexuality and homosexuality (DeWinter *et al.*, 2015; Gilmour, Schalomon, and Smith, 2011). Our interviews also reflected what we discovered in the research. Many of the participants said that they saw people as people and not through the lens of gender; that they're attracted to the person and not the gender. It's possible that having ASD makes a person more flexible in who they're attracted to, just from a neurological standpoint.

All in all, there seems to be enough evidence to indicate that individuals with ASD tend to be more divergent in their gender identity and sexual orientation than their non-ASD counterparts (DeWinter *et al.*, 2015; Gilmour, *et al.*, 2011; Janssen *et al.*, 2016; for more on prevalence rates, see research in Chapter 1). According to researchers, this may be so due to the synergistic interaction of biological factors such as hormones, neurochemicals, and social factors ways that are unique to being on the autism spectrum (George and Stokes, 2016).

Meredith: Research on this very question has been widespread in recent years and will likely continue. As Eva shared, there have been studies contesting the idea that there is a higher prevalence of transgender and LGBTQ individuals within the autism community, and vice versa. One article (Turban and van Schalkwyk, 2018) points out valid critiques of the way prior articles have measured gender diversity and autism within their samples, and questions this link. We will continue to learn about these intersecting identities as more people investigate this. Regardless of the prevalence rates, it is important to listen to the voices of those living at the intersection. In this book, as well as in a study I did on the experiences of being transgender and autistic, participants shared that they talk about the high number of their friends who are also LGBTQ and autistic, and wonder about the connection between the identities. It is important to focus on the experience of those who are living at the intersection of LGBTQ and autistic identities, as many are out there, and most providers are not equipped to support them.

2. Is the experience of an ASD-LGBTQ individual different from that of a non-autistic LGBTQ Individual?

Eva: Well, ASD is a social, communication, and emotions-based difference in addition to often being a developmental delay. Due to their social-communication-emotional challenges, many autistic individuals struggle to make friends and many tend to be loners in their developing years. Due to the developmental delay, they may also experience puberty and adolescence, at least mentally and emotionally, at an older age. Therefore, they may not have peers to gain gender-and-sexuality-related information from and may also have a delayed awareness of their own body and sexuality, ASD individuals may often discover their identities at a later stage then their non-ASD peers.

For example, some ASD-LGBTQ individuals report that they didn't necessarily have words or language for their felt-identity, and that this was a major challenge, as stated here:

> I didn't have the labels for what I was until later. It wasn't until I met other people who were like me and said "that is my experience." A lot of nubius thoughts about things but not necessarily as concrete until later. (Hillier *et al.*, 2018)

However once they come out to themselves, they may not be as beholden to what their peers think of them in the way that most non-ASD individuals are. They may also have friends who are similarly neurodiverse or divergent, so they may feel more accepted by peers who are more or less similar to them. Due to the fact that ASD individuals aren't as aware of societal conventions, they might also feel less anxious and more free to explore their gender identity and sexual orientation. On the other hand, if they have anxiety and depression, which are common comorbid features of ASD (Strang *et al.*, 2012) they may overanalyze and be wrecked with self-doubt upon discovery. Experiences of ASD individuals can also be highly variable in that each person with ASD is very unique.

Autistic individuals tend not to follow strict gender roles and rules, even when they are cishet. Of course, this is not an absolute rule, and some autistic adults may adopt exaggerated male or female physical traits. However, many ASD individuals, even when they are from a particular culture, tend not to adhere to cultural gender stereotypes. For example, one of my clients who lives in India, a culture with somewhat defined gender roles, helps out his wife with childcare and cooks the majority of his family's meals, so much so that even friends and family members think this to be unusual, but it doesn't stop them from enjoying the freedom that comes with not being defined by cultural gender roles.

Even when divergent in gender and orientation, autistic individuals tend to "live gender" differently. They are often less binary and more imbuing of both masculine and feminine qualities in their gender presentation (Brody, 2016; Bumiller, 2008). They are also not as motivated by societal norms, perhaps due to their trait of being less cognizant of nonverbal cues and the hidden curriculum of social behavior. There might also be a correlation to the fact that they are often more focused on their special interests and intellectual pursuits.

It's easier to ignore or not notice social rules when one is enjoying being immersed in one's own passions and interests.

That said, while having special interests and not being as tuned into social norms may make them less vulnerable to prejudice and discrimination than their non-autistic LGBTQ peers, they're also likely to be more vulnerable due to the fact that they may not be accepted by the LGBTQ communities (see Chapter 17, *Partner Perspective—Violet*). Having multiple identities can mean having really contradictory experiences and it can also be difficult to find those who truly "get" one's experience.

Another aspect that's difficult for ASD-LGBTQ individuals and ASD individuals in general is that they have trouble developing and maintaining friends and support networks, so loneliness can be a major challenge for those on the spectrum, but once again this isn't always the case as we've seen in our participants—most of them have developed and worked hard to establish strong support networks.

Meredith: As highlighted by Eva, there are some differences in the ways one's autistic identity may intersect with LGBTQ identity. However, there are also parallels in experience of identity development, awareness, and finding a label that fits which I've observed across both autistic and non-autistic individuals. In addition, the factors that help non-autistic LGBTQ individuals be resilient are also likely to be the same for autistic individuals. For example, being accepted by family members and/or having a support system have been found to be supportive for LGBTQ individuals (D'amico *et al.*, 2015), and emerging research suggests this is the case for those who are autistic and transgender (Maroney and Horne, 2018).

Due to the traits that are often associated with ASD which Eva mentioned, autistic LGBTQ individuals may have difficulty finding a community of support within the general LGBTQ community, and in sub-groups of the community, which tend to be the social hubs. For instance, sexual minority individuals historically depended on gay bars as a way of socializing with others in a venue that is safe and accessible (Rotello and Gillis, 1997). Connecting with others in a bar setting may not fit for autistic LGBTQ people, particularly when considering the sensory overload that an autistic person may experience in a space that is very crowded, noisy, with the potential for loud music and bright lights.

3. When it comes to gender identity and sexual orientation, do ASD individuals mimic people in their peer group or what they see in social media?

Eva: Like I said in response to the question above, many people with ASD gravitate to friends and peers who have similar profiles. That said, so far, I haven't met anyone who was just mimicking their friends or what they saw in the media. On rare occasions, I have met clients who may have questioned their gender identity and sexual orientation for a very brief period of time, but it seems that their questioning phase didn't seem to last too long. I once had a young man attend my Gender Identity Support group because he was questioning; however, he never returned and when I ran into him at a social event almost a year later, he pulled me aside and mentioned how he'd been questioning when he attended the group, but after attending the group, he realized that he didn't quite identify with the rest of the participants and that he now identifies as cishet.

So, I do think that it's important that all people have the flexibility and freedom to explore their gender identity and sexual orientation even if they don't end up identifying as divergent in the end.

4. I've heard that autistic people are unable to understand and identify their own sexual orientation and gender identity. Is that true?

Eva: Yes, I've heard this too. Frankly, in my own experience, in all the time that I've worked with autistic adults, I've yet to meet someone who was unable to understand or identify their sexual orientation and gender identity, or is confused about it in some way. It may be true that ASD may delay an individual's understanding or acceptance of their gender identity and sexual orientation, but an autistic person still knows who they are and who they're attracted to. So, I'm inclined to think it's a myth.

Even when intellectually impaired, I'm inclined to believe that an autistic person understands their gender and orientation. For example, one of the core participants in my support group was a very visibly autistic individual with a less-than-average, or what is known as a borderline, IQ, and a significant speech impediment. Even though she struggled to articulate at times, she was aware of her identity as a trans woman. She absolutely delighted in being correctly gendered and was so visibly happy when the group supported her in using the name she had chosen for herself. She also took great pride in her developing feminine appearance with laser hair removal, which she told us she'd been working on for a couple of years. She was also fortunate in that she had the support of her family and her therapist, who was an ASD-gender identity specialist.

Meredith: As expressed by our participants, autistic people are able to identify their sexual orientation and gender identity. In some cases, they may experience less distress doing so as they may not be internalizing cishet norms in the same manner as non-autistic LGBTQ individuals. Finding a space that is accepting to disclose these identities may be more challenging for autistic individuals, but the greater accessibility of online groups, communities, and message boards may be making this easier for individuals. Many autistic LGBTQ people that I've talked to had an internal sense that they were different than their cishet peers in some way, but did not have the language to describe their sexual orientation or gender identity. As Alyia (see Chapter 15) put it: "the Internet is your friend. Don't jump into any predefined boxes up front." By speaking with other LGBTQ individuals or posting online, many are finding ways to label and describe their identity in these spaces. Finding a way to describe identity, similar to a diagnosis, can be very empowering for some people, and also may decrease feelings of being alone or the only one.

5. What sorts of challenges may someone who identifies as LGBTQ and ASD encounter?

Meredith: Autistic people may experience discrimination when coming out as LGBTQ, above and beyond that experienced by their non-spectrum counterparts. There are a number of societal factors that may be related to this. For instance, there are misconceptions that autistic individuals are all asexual, which may be true for some, but there is incredible diversity in identity, as evidenced by our participants. Furthermore, there is general avoidance of considering anyone with a disability as a sexual being, which can be another barrier for autistic individuals. Some autistic individuals may face others questioning their capability to identify their sexual orientation or gender identity just because they are on the autism spectrum. Traits commonly associated with autism can also be used against individuals expressing diversity in sexual orientation or gender identity, by labeling it as a special interest, something that is common for those on the autism spectrum.

The difficulty of finding providers that are knowledgeable about, and affirming to, autistic and LGBTQ individuals can be a major barrier to care. Many face discrimination within healthcare settings, such as being misgendered or having their identity dismissed. Others may fail to disclose their sexual orientation or gender identity out of fear of negative consequences or discrimination, which can also be problematic for their health and overall well-being. As we've seen in the literature on general LGBTQ individuals, openness with primary care providers about sexual orientation and gender identity has been found to be associated with better health outcomes (Clark *et al.*, 2017). When people are comfortable talking with these providers about their identities, their care is able to be more tailored to them, and those who are knowledgeable use this knowledge to make preventative decisions, such as education around sexual health.

Eva: That's so true. Basically, autistic LGBTQ individuals have to contend with the challenges of being both autistic and LGBTQ. These are two major identities that are pervasive and there are parallels to being LGBTQ and ASD. However, it's not the same for everyone. If someone is trans, then their experience may be different than someone who's gay. So, it's really a case-by-case situation. But there are certain challenges that people face that are more universal. For example, the social issues are still there whatever the gender and orientation. For example, one of my lesbian clients once stated: "I don't know how to ask women out. I think I come on too strong and can creep people out." As for gay autistic men, they report not fitting into the stereotypical gay social culture and may not be accepted by the gay community. Autistic individuals can sometimes also be more naive and vulnerable and emotionally younger, so they might be more susceptible to being taken advantage of.

It can be difficult for some individuals with autism to make ends meet financially, due to their ASD traits, but having an LGBTQ identity in addition to ASD can create additional obstacles, especially if either aspect of the individual's identity is more obvious. A lot seems to depend on where one lives and one's socioeconomic status. For example, Yaeli (see Chapter 9) reports that her workplace has been very accepting of both of her identities, but she works in a high-tech company and has a high-paying/high-skilled job. While we've seen in Alyia's story (Chapter 15), due to her highly obvious trans woman identity, it's become more difficult for her to get work as an arborist.

6. We know one distinguishing feature of ASD is sensory issues. Does this play a role in their ASD-LGBTQ overlap as well?

Eva: In general, even without being gender and orientation divergent, autistic people can often have severe sensory problems. They can be over- and/or under-sensitive to noise, light, clothing, texture, touch, or temperature. Basically, their five senses—of sight, hearing, touch, smell, and taste—let in either too much or too little information from their environment.

Often "body dysphoria can be a sensory assault and people may 'stim' to endure dysphoria and neural overload" (Brody, 2016). Body dysphoria can be a major challenge for someone on the spectrum as people with ASD can often be overly sensitive to visual stimuli, so having to endure the way one looks vs. the way one imagines oneself can be rather excruciating and traumatic. Not being in the body that they want to be in can also create a lot of mental strain, sensory disturbance, and destabilization. For example, one of my clients who identifies as non-binary and asexual said that they just didn't like how their breasts "felt" and that they were able to dramatically reduce their mental stress once they had breast removal surgery.

Another client who had trouble "sensing themselves in their body" reported "being so in my head that I always feel like I'm always floating four inches above my body and so I think that this mind-body disconnect has had an impact on how I understand my gender on a more visceral level."

A trans woman client once reported that she had trouble finding feminine clothes that didn't itch or cause her terrible discomfort during her coming-out phase because she was so used to wearing jeans and t-shirts without labels and tags. Ultimately, she settled on wearing jeans and t-shirts as a trans woman as well; she just chose ones that felt more feminine and "girly" to her.

Others can struggle with taste, touch, and smell when engaging in a sexual activity, or when sharing physical affection with their partner. Therefore, along with their partner, they may have to figure out strategies to accommodate their sensory sensitivities. For example, a client of mine has severe sensory dysregulation due to work stress. Feeling so out of sorts with her body can then make her feel spaced out and not very present to her wife, even in their intimate moments. She learned that an intense power yoga class can give her that intense muscle burn, deep joint pressure, and the physical and emotional grounding that she needs in order to feel more in sync with her wife in bed.

7. Is an ASD diagnosis necessary for individuals on the spectrum?

Eva: Getting an ASD assessment can be a huge challenge. Providers who specialize in ASD, may not be informed about LGBTQ identities; and those who are trained and experienced in the LGBTQ population may not know about ASD. So, it can be difficult to find providers who understand the overlap of LGBTQ identities and ASD. As we've seen in the interviews, so many individuals were diagnosed with ASD as adults and then too it might have been a journey with many false starts and misdiagnoses. A lack of a proper diagnosis can often pile on additional stress to individuals already grappling with gender and orientation issues.

The dual identity of ASD-LGBTQ can cause many medical professionals to question one or the other identity. Many ASD-LGBTQ individuals report being disappointed by doctors and mental health professionals because the clinician may dismiss their LGBTQ identity or question it based on the fact that they're ASD (Hillier *et al.*, 2018). Many professionals may even attribute being LGBTQ to being ASD or take people on the spectrum less seriously. So, not only is getting an ASD diagnosis difficult, but individuals also have to prove themselves to be legitimately LGBTQ!

I think that self-diagnosis for ASD is just as valid as a formal diagnosis, especially for adults, as attested by some of our participants. That said, as we've seen for our participants, their parents and partners, a formal diagnosis or discussion on diagnosis with an ASD specialist was also deeply validating. Many people feel a deep sense of relief to know why they are the way they are and that it's not that they're "just bad at life," or are "being deliberately difficult," or "mean" and "lazy." Having an accurate diagnosis can mean getting the right treatment in terms of psychotherapy and sometimes medication.

Learning specific ASD-related tips and strategies and having employment or school/college accommodations can greatly enhance the ability to succeed in life. For example, after her diagnosis with me, one of my clients went on to get a specially trained Autism Service Animal that helps her with her social anxiety and meltdowns in unexpected public situations by interrupting her behavior and guiding her back to her car or to a quiet space. This has markedly improved my client's life as she's a professional, wife, and mother. Having a formal diagnosis therefore allowed this young woman to spend less time recovering from her disorienting and distressing social anxiety and often public meltdowns.

Often a diagnosis can save a couple's relationship because without the ASD framework, the non-ASD partner is likely to think that their partner just doesn't care about them or is being knowingly cruel. Both Aliya and Maya's partners (Chapter 16 and 17, respectively) explained how knowing about ASD greatly helped them to understand their ASD partner and the motivations behind their behaviors.

8. What advice do you have for someone who's autistic and wants to explore their gender identity or sexual orientation?

Meredith: Trust yourself as the expert on your own experiences. Find safe spaces to talk with others who have navigated this before, whether it is online or in person. There are so many great resources for anyone who is exploring their gender identity or sexual orientation. There are also forums and groups with others talking about what their process of identity awareness and development looked like. This is a unique time for LGBTQ people, particularly those living in rural areas. It is possible to follow YouTubers' gender confirmation or social transition or to connect with young queer people sharing their stories, which can be a major source of inspiration and support for those in the early stages of exploration.

Eva: As mentioned previously by Meredith and many of our participants, there are many online avenues these days to start out with. Reading and learning as much as you can about your gender and/or orientation might be the first step.

The second step might be coming out to your family, if you think that they will be supportive. There are ways of finding out if they would be, with subtle hints and hypothetical questions. If one's family isn't supportive, then the second step might be finding supportive and accepting communities like an ASD-LGBTQ support group and ASD-specific organizations such as the Asperger/Autism Network,[1] which might be able to lead you to counseling and support groups in the community.

The third step might be finding an ASD-LGBTQ specialist or even just an LGBTQ specialist to begin with. Please find another therapist if the one you go to isn't affirming or doesn't believe you.

Finally, it's very important to find like-minded individuals for friendships, partnerships, and relationships (romantic, sexual, or otherwise), so that you have the right kinds of support and are living the life you want and will enjoy.

9. What advice do you have for parents of an autistic person who's exploring or questioning their gender identity or sexual orientation?

Meredith: I agree with a lot of what Eva shared. You may have a variety of reactions, but try your best to understand what it was like for your child to share this part of themselves with you, and how they may be feeling. Be supportive. Validate their experience. Educate yourself. Talk with other parents of LGBTQ youth. Consider reaching out to your local PFLAG[2] to answer any questions you may have, and to learn how to best support your child. It is normal to worry about your child, and many parents have the worry that their child's life with be that much more difficult if they are LGBTQ. For instance, in a study that interviewed mothers of transgender children diagnosed with ASD, parents reflected on their worries about their children growing up in a transphobic and cisnormative society, even when they were accepting, as well as the challenges finding adequate support for their children (Kuvalanka *et al.*, 2017). If your child is school-aged, you may find yourself needing to educate others and advocate for your child. There are some great stories out there of parents who share their own stories of supporting their kids. It may also be helpful to find to find communities of support for you as a parent, depending on your child's age.

Family support is invaluable for LGBTQ youth, and can actually be protective from some negative experiences. Youth who experience

1 www.AANE.org
2 www.pflag.org

family support are more comfortable coming out with their sexual orientation, and have more positive mental and physical health and overall well-being (D'amico *et al.*, 2015; D'Augelli, 2002; Shilo and Savaya, 2011). Also, transgender youth with better family functioning have been found to have better individual mental health outcomes (Katz-Wise *et al.*, 2018). Those who experience family rejection of their sexual orientation and gender identity may experience negative impacts such as increased depression, risky sexual behaviors, suicide attempts, and substance misuse (Bradford *et al.*, 2013; D'Augelli, 2002; Klein and Golub, 2016; Ryan *et al.*, 2009). Some individuals may not receive outright rejection for coming out, but rather will experience heterosexism/transphobia from their family-of-origin through invalidation of their identities, exclusion from family events, or heterosexist, transphobic, or homophobic comments. These more subtle rejections can also negatively impact the physical and mental health of LGBTQ individuals (Jefferson, Neilands and Sevelius, 2013; Zakalik and Wei, 2006), which is important to consider.

Eva: I agree with a lot of what Meredith shared. We've seen two interviews of healthy and supportive parents in this book, and it's ideal when parents are able to be supportive of their children as they go through this journey. As Meredith noted as well, studies have been very clear that LGBTQ people who are rejected by their families have poorer physical health and are more likely to take risks like having unprotected sex and using drugs (Ryan, 2009). Family rejection and/or even having to hide one's identity from family can also lead to lower self-esteem and self-worth as well as isolation and having fewer people to turn to in the event of a crisis.

Therefore, it's absolutely crucial that parents take the initiative to educate themselves and understand about the ASD-LGBTQ intersecting identities and are able to accept and support their decisions. Of course, for some parents to be supportive, they might need resources and encouragement through attending parent support groups, seminars, and workshops, and receiving counseling as well. It's important that parents get the support and information they need to support their child from sources *other* than their child. For many families, this is not an easy journey, so the more help everyone can get, the better off they're likely to be.

I think really listening to your child would be the first step—truly being there for them, supporting and encouraging them as they explore their gender and/or orientation. It is important to continue to demonstrate your unconditional love, even if you find yourself initially struggling with it all. Reading and learning as much as you can about gender and/or orientation would also be helpful. Nowadays, there are a lot of online resources, books, and even research articles out there.

Know that you're not alone: there are many other parents out there who are in a similar situation to you. Join support groups and speak to other parents who can provide you with more perspective and understanding. It's okay to be confused and upset, but please seek help with a psychotherapist for this, because you don't want to process your distress with your child. They have enough to deal with as it is.

If certain family members and friends aren't supportive, you may have to try to inform and educate them; but if they continue to be unaccepting and critical, then you might need to use your wisdom and either meet them without your child for a while, while continuing to dialogue with them as, just like you, they may also need time to process this. Of course, if relatives act hostile or destructive, then it might be best to keep your distance from them. You're not to blame for your offspring's orientation or gender. This is not a reflection on you. Some things just are, and your child has a unique mission and purpose in the world; help them live it!

10. Any suggestions for individuals coming out to their friends and family?

Eva: It seems like coming out for many people isn't just a one-time thing. It can be an ongoing, multi-layered process, especially for those with multiple identities. Each family and set of parents and siblings are different, so depending on the family one comes from, I suppose one might need to test the waters and see how coming out would be received by one's relatives. There are a lot of online and offline LGBTQ communities out there that might help in how to go about coming out, whether to friends or family. Speaking to a qualified therapist about the best way to approach the situation might also be useful, especially for those on the spectrum who have high anxiety or who may have more close-minded families. One may need to work out various scenarios of how to approach coming out to their family or friends. Once there is sufficient support from a therapist, friends, and/or a partner, one can gain the courage and confidence needed to come out and this journey will become easier in time.

Meredith: The experience of coming out can really differ with sexual orientation and gender identity. Eva highlighted a pretty common misconception, which is that coming out is a one-time experience. The reality is that individuals are coming out multiple times, and that the experience of coming out as gay or lesbian is very different than someone who is choosing to either conceal or disclose their transgender identity (Rood *et al.*, 2017). There are real safety concerns for people to consider depending on their context. That's why I would encourage anyone to explore this with a therapist, friend, family members and to access resources online, such as the Trevor Project: Coming Out As You[3] or the Human Rights Coming Out Center[4] to name a few examples.

It is also important to consider other intersecting identities, such as race/ethnicity or religious community, as this might change a person's decision about whether or not it is safe for them to come out. For instance, the experience of someone who is a white, cisgender, gay man and chooses to come out to family may be significantly different than that of a black, transgender woman. Individuals should reflect on their own familial or living experiences and talk with other supportive people about the expectations from their family or living situation, particularly if they are a young person and are still living at home. LGBTQ young people have high rates of homelessness, often due to family rejection after coming out. For some, the experience of coming out is very positive, and one that often leads to better mental health outcomes, especially for lesbian, bisexual, and queer individuals. The decision to come out as trans is often more complex—some people may prefer to conceal details about their history, or aim to pass as male or female, in which case coming out may not be their preferred choice, particularly depending on the setting.

---

3 www.thetrevorproject.org/about/programs-services/coming-out-as-you

4 www.hrc.org/coming-out-center#.WuijM9PwaRs

11. What do you suggest a person do when their friends or family aren't supportive of their LGBTQ identity?

Meredith: Unfortunately this can happen, which may result in a lot of feelings of hurt and anger in the person who has been rejected by family or friends. I would encourage anyone who has experienced this to take care of yourself, by seeking out individual therapy or group therapy support, and by processing this loss with those who have been supportive of your identity. It may also be helpful to seek out spaces that you find validating to your LGBTQ identity, whether it is through a shared interest, events for LGBTQ people, or those who share similar beliefs. Many LGBTQ individuals create families of choice, sometimes in addition to their family of origin, to get support, validation, and care from a community of people who accept them.

Eva: When family or friends aren't supportive, I'd say find new like-minded friends who you can rely on; and it's okay to keep trying until you land with the right group of close friends and confidants. ASD often means that one can struggle to develop and create friendships; therefore, one may have to work harder to make friends, but it is vital that this be given importance as life can be harder without the right kinds of support. That said, most of the participants in the book seem to have created pretty good support systems for themselves in the form of alternative communities, friendships with similarly identified peers, counselors, and romantic partners. Some have even worked hard to bridge the gap with family members. In addition, conferences and workshops, Pride events, ASD-related forums and events, and even special interest groups can also serve as safe, accepting, and affirming communities.

As far as family goes, I imagine every situation is a little bit different. I'd say, please reach out to therapists and support groups to discuss your situation so that they can provide the support that might be lacking from your family members and discuss how you can advocate for yourself. Know that some parents may just need more time to come around; don't give up on someday having a better relationship with family members. Of course, this might not be the advice for everyone, especially if family continues to have a detrimental effect on you. That said, working on family relationships can be a lifelong thing, so if you're getting a lot of judgment and negativity from your relatives, it's very important to take care and protect yourself, and even to maintain distance if you have to.

12. What advice do you have for partners of ASD-LGBTQ individuals?

Eva: As a couples counselor specializing in couples where one or both partners might be on the spectrum, I can say that many ASD relationships are fraught with challenges. So, if you're having difficulties in your relationship, I'd recommend reading up about ASD and relationships and marriage. There's a lot of information out there in the form of blogs, articles, and books.

My book, *Marriage and Lasting Relationships with Asperger's Syndrome* (Mendes 2015), is pretty comprehensive about what to expect in a relationship with a partner with ASD and the strategies and tools to deal with it. There are a couple of case studies in there pertaining to lesbian couples, but regardless of gender and orientation, the strategies and tools seem to be helpful to a majority of couples where one partner is on the spectrum.

It's really important to understand ASD traits and how they manifest in a relationship, so that the non-ASD partner doesn't take a lot of things that their Aspie partner does or doesn't do, personally. It's also important for the partner with ASD to understand their own traits and how they affect their partner. Helping them become more self-aware and encouraging them to work on this can make a big difference.

An Aspie partner may not always know how to meet your needs, hence you might also need a good support system of your own in the form of close friends, family, support groups, and therapists. Depending on your partner's particular traits and need for accommodations, you may both have to learn how to adapt to each other's needs. If there are mental health issues present, often for both partners, make sure you both get the care and help you need. Many couples, regardless of orientation, seek out couples counseling when it's too late in the relationship, so going to an ASD-specialist counselor as soon as the trouble begins brewing is a good idea.

13. What about support for partners of those who might be exploring or questioning their gender identity or sexual orientation?

Meredith: There are a number of resources out there for partners of individuals who are exploring their gender identity and/or sexual orientation. It is important to communicate openly, seek out resources and support, and to determine how the couple wishes to navigate this experience together. There are therapy or support groups, online platforms, and personal accounts and books for partners of individuals who are exploring a transgender identity.[5]

If possible, it may be helpful to seek out the support of a couples therapist who is experienced in supporting clients through this process as they determine their new identities as individuals, and as a couple. It can be a challenging journey as one person is exploring a part of their identity that will, more often than not, impact the couple as a system. Seeking out support from others who have navigated this, as well as experienced providers, may be helpful.

Eva: For many people, having their partner explore or question their gender and/or orientation can be a shocking and traumatic experience. As Meredith said, seeing a therapist who specializes in this area is an important first step, as well as accessing resources in the form of books, online forums, and support groups for straight partners of gay, lesbian, and bisexual partners. Many relationships may not be able to survive such an transformation. That said, since the LGBTQ spectrum is so broad, I think every couple's situation is unique, therefore this is a complex and difficult question to answer. Jessica Kingsley Publishers has a portfolio of books on the ASD-LGBTQ experience that might be a huge support for someone whose partner might be questioning or seeking to transition their gender identity.

14. How can providers such as therapists, counselors, psychologists, psychiatrists, primary care-physicians, and other clinicians provide affirming care?

Meredith: At the most basic level, use your clinical skills and training to simply listen to your clients or patients, and trust them as the expert

5 See this website for a comprehensive list: www.transgenderpartners.com/resource-for-partners-2.

on their own experiences. It is a good idea to seek out additional training if you find yourself working with clients who are LGBTQ and autistic, particularly to learn about language that is affirming, and to empower you as the provider to ask the right questions. Although you may be familiar with LGBTQ terminology or diagnostic criteria for autism, it is important to understand the way your clients make sense of their identities or choose to label their experience.

It's also important to avoid making assumptions about what the client needs from you. For example, although an autistic client may come out to you as queer, they may be interested in focusing on skills related to job readiness, rather than processing their identity. By asking what your client needs, you can provide focused treatment and determine ways to be the most helpful, whether it is advocating with or for your client, or connecting them to additional services. On the other hand, an autistic person may be struggling to navigate the process of seeking gender confirmation services, which may require you to first learn about it in order to provide psychoeducation.

Eva: Going from my own experiences, I was assigned to work with clients who were ASD-LGBTQ at the very beginning of my counseling career, starting from when I was in graduate school and interning at the Asperger/Autism Network (AANE). My very first ASD client when I was an intern was an androgynous-appearing older woman who later revealed to me that she might be bisexual. So right from the get go, when I was just learning about ASD, I was fortunate enough to see clients with these intersecting identities. At the time, having a beginner's mind really helped me connect with my clients and I don't think that has really changed for me. I would say that almost everything I've learned about the ASD-LGBTQ overlap, I've learned from my clients and soaked up things they've told me about themselves. I really learned to see the world through their perspective. Of course, I've also read research papers, articles, and books, watched many documentaries, and also participated in workshops, conferences, and webinars on ASD as well as LGBTQ. I'm also fortunate to have close friends and colleagues who are LGBTQ who have helped me grow and expand both as a clinician and person.

My advice for other clinicians while working with ASD-LGBTQ individuals would be to learn all about ASD and also then about gender and orientation. And then keep an open mind and just listen to your clients or patients and trust what they say. They are the experts on their lives, so don't second guess or doubt them. Don't assume that you know more about your client than they do, in any regard. Become aware of and actively work on eliminating your own biases and prejudices. If you feel uncomfortable working with certain clients and are struggling to work with them, then it might be best to refer them to a specialist in the ASD-LGBTQ area.

Adjust your intake forms to include spaces for preferred pronouns and names. If the client isn't coming in for LGBTQ-related issues, then it's better not to bring it up unless they do. At the same time, it's crucial to create a safe space with your own mindset, body language, and attitude, so that if the client feels like it's something they need to discuss, they feel free and comfortable to do so.

Perhaps due to my ASD specialization, many of my dual-identity ASD-LGBTQ clients come to me for ASD-related challenges. Unless the client wants to discuss the LGBTQ-related issues, it's not necessarily a starting point for our work. The topic of their LGBTQ identity usually comes out in the context of their relationship, employment, family, sensory, or life issues and then we go from there... For every session, the client is the one who sets the agenda in terms of what's discussed. That way, I can be sure that I'm meeting my clients' needs.

Also, if you don't know something or haven't heard of a particular term, it's okay to admit not knowing. It's important to apologize to the client if necessary for any reason. Autistic clients might not be the best at providing feedback to the therapist and there may be times when the therapist might be wondering if they're being helpful or not. To this effect, I wanted to share a quote by my former supervisor who trained me in working with autistic adults. When I asked her, "How will I know if my clients like me?" she quipped, "If you like them, they will like you!" Alternatively, you could ask if the client feels like they are being helped.

15. Is self-disclosure to my employer or workplace recommended?

Eva: Disclosure in the workplace can be a fraught decision. I've worked with numerous clients where they've successfully disclosed their ASD status to their employers in order to request specific accommodations that would help them do better at their jobs. I start by asking my clients what they want the employer to know with regard to their disability and how it might relate to their job description. For example, a client of mine, who worked in technology, needed to be excused from the many meetings that she was required to be in. I met with her for an official diagnosis and provided her with a disclosure letter requesting her employer to reduce the number of meetings she was required to attend due to her challenges in transitioning from meetings and then having trouble focusing on the coding aspect of her job. Her supervisor was supportive and her request was granted, which has now allowed her to excel at her programing work.

In an ideal situation, in a work environment, it would be best if the individual could fully be themselves in terms of gender and orientation. That said, we don't live in an ideal world, and therefore disclosing your LGBTQ identity to your employer can be fraught and it is important to carefully weigh the situation. In some cases, disclosure may mean discrimination or even danger, which may mean that the individual might have to keep their LGBTQ identity or identities at a low profile at work. Some work environments are more supportive than others, for example, one of my clients worked in a cafe owned by a lesbian couple who employed primarily LGBTQ staff. In his case, his identity as a trans man was actually an advantage in his workplace as he fit in very well with his coworkers. It's important to know your social setting and carefully consider whether disclosure is necessary.

For many LGBTQ people, their identities are more visible and so they can't really hide who they are. In such cases, it's important to choose a place of work that is safe and accepting and consider changing jobs if one feels like one's in a job environment that is intolerant or dangerous.

Also, it's best to carefully discuss disclosure with family, friends, a therapist, or even a legal consultant, who might be able to guide you through the self-disclosure process at work.

16. What suggestions do you have for someone thinking of transitioning?

Meredith: For those who are considering gender confirmation surgery or hormone therapy, I would recommend doing some research on your rights (by state or country), as well as on the interventions you are interested in. There are a number of individuals who are increasingly sharing their stories of transition on platforms like YouTube or Instagram, who choose to post their experience, as well as thoughts and feelings that come up for them during this process. It can be beneficial to talk with others about their experience of navigating the healthcare system, as this can often be a barrier for people; this could be particularly helpful if you live in the same area and would like a first-hand account of what it was like to work with a doctor or provider.

There are great guidelines online, which I would encourage individuals to review and ensure that their provider has reviewed the recommendations for working with transgender and gender non-conforming people who are seeking out medical intervention as part of their transition. The World Professional Association for Transgender Health (WPATH)[6] is one great resource that I would recommend sharing with providers, while Fenway Health[7] has accessible information for those who are considering hormone therapy and might have questions. In addition, you might prefer seeking out a provider that advertises competence in working with transgender patients, if that is possible in your area. It still may be important for you to talk with others who have navigated services, to find the best fit for you. There are also great books and articles that we have come across that may help. Choosing to transition medically is not something everyone wants to pursue. Many people will choose to socially transition, which many find to be a good option for them, and could include going by a different name or pronouns, changing their appearance (e.g. their clothes, haircut or accessories), or choosing to use a different restroom.

Eva: As we've seen in our participants, not every transgender person seeks to transition physically, but many do. In full disclosure, while I've seen many trans individuals for counseling, it has been primarily for their ASD-related life and relationship challenges; therefore, I haven't been that involved in the letter-writing approval process for my clients. That said, I've supported clients prior to or post transition and sometimes even during, and the issues below seem to have come up for many of them.

6 www.wpath.org/publications/soc
7 http://fenwayhealth.org/care/medical/transgender-health

Medical gatekeepers

It seems like medical gatekeepers can be a big challenge. My clients tell me that often when there's a dual diagnosis of ASD and body dysmorphia, the therapists or doctors involved don't take them seriously and treat them as if their ASD disables them from knowing their gender.

"Gatekeeper" is a term that evolved from the process of the trans patient having to "undergo extensive talk therapy in order to access medical interventions" (Urquhart, 2016), as transgender individuals are required to obtain a letter written by their therapist to receive services (Budge, 2015). The gatekeeper—often the therapist writing the letter—was the one that made the ultimate decision about who was or was not a candidate for treatments ranging from hormones to surgery (Urquhart, 2016). However, more recently, trans advocates have made the point against this system of red tape and gatekeeping and are instead favoring a system of "informed consent" in which the patient is given information and educated about the treatments and risks involved, but the end decision of treatment choices is made by the patient alone (Urquhart, 2016).

This gatekeeping process has thus been exhausting, draining, and intimidating for many of the people I've spoken to. Also, the social-communication challenges individuals with ASD may experience make them more vulnerable to the fact that the therapist may misunderstand them and reach the wrong conclusions about them. Therefore it would be good to seek out working with a therapist specializing in ASD-LGBTQ. Having a friend, family member, or partner accompany you to sessions to interpret and support you as you advocate for yourself might also be important.

Research

As with any life-altering procedure, doing a fair amount of research and seeking out treatments from reputable specialists also seems important. One of my clients who transitioned mentioned that they had sought counsel from a couple of well-known specialists in helping them transition.

Clear Communications

Properly communicating what one desires in one's anatomy is another important aspect of transitioning—I've had a client who struggled to properly communicate with their surgeon about their breast size for example. The surgeon didn't fully understand the exact nature of what the patient was looking for and ended up giving her breasts that were a couple of sizes bigger than she wanted. Of course, this was a fixable situation, but it still meant an extra financial investment and a physical toll in terms of additional modification surgery. Therefore, being crystal clear and going over the details many times might be beneficial, as is also having a trusted friend, family member, or ally with you whilst consulting with the physician.

17. Do you have any thoughts on safety issues for ASD and LGBTQ individuals?

Eva: Safety is definitely a major issue in the LGBTQ community. Being ASD and LGBTQ can create a sort of double jeopardy for people because they may not always sense or know when they are in dangerous territory due to their naivete and lack of social awareness. They may also not be able to intuit if someone is being genuinely nice to them or trying to take advantage of them, until it's a little too late.

Living in a particular part of the country or the world can also be dangerous, and not everyone has a choice in where to live, so it can be difficult to live authentically in some instances. Education, financial stability, and family support are also important safety factors. The more highly educated a person is, the more financial stability they're bound to have and therefore the more choices they will have about how and where they live, and access to accepting and inclusive communities. Also, having a supportive family can be a tremendous benefit. This cannot be underestimated.

Race is also an influence in how safe an LGBTQ person is. Being a person of color with LGBTQ increases the risk of being killed (Steinmetz, 2017). To quote Nijah, our participant who is African American, and male and female (Chapter 3):

> It can be dangerous to tell others. However, I'm not saying this to scare you. I say keep it to yourself (especially if you're LGBTQ) from your family until you can stand on your own two feet without help

> from any of them, because the moment they find out, they may cut you off.

Another example is that I once had a black participant in my support group who wanted to talk about his grandmother being concerned about him visiting his friend in a predominantly white neighborhood. He downplayed the risk involved until I described to him how his grandmother did have a point in that he could potentially find himself in the wrong place at the wrong time and could hypothetically be at risk from the police. So, I think it's important to gauge danger and discuss the situation with a friend or family member or a therapist. That said, these discussions should be had on a case-by-case basis, as everyone's situation is unique.

My clients who are white, gay, or lesbian and who can pass as male or female even if they identify as non-binary or genderfluid seem to have the least safety issues. Also, a lot of my clients live in parts of the country that are more tolerant and accepting of openly LGBTQ individuals. Therefore, living in an LGBTQ-friendly community might be something to consider.

Trans individuals seem to be the most at-risk group even within the LGBTQ community. Suicide rates are high for the trans population as it is and, tragically, so are homicide rates (Steinmetz, 2017; Virupaksha, Muralidhar and Ramakrishna, 2016).

There's a good book by Liane Holliday Willey called *Safety Skills for Asperger Women* (2012) that covers a broad range of safety topics related to being female and on the spectrum.

Finally, the last thing I want to say about safety is that it's very important to have allies wherever one goes. An "ally" is a term used to describe someone who is supportive of LGBTQ people. It encompasses non-LGBTQ allies as well as those within the LGBTQ community who support each other (e.g. a lesbian who is an ally to the bisexual community) (Miller, 2015).

Know who your allies are and make sure you have lots of them in your place of work, within your friendship circle, as part of support groups, psychotherapists, LGBTQ and/or ASD-related organizations, and even neighbors. It's important to have a group of trustworthy individuals who you can really rely on and count on to not only understand and accept you, but also stand up for you, protect, and defend you when needed.

18. What advice do you have for someone looking for an ASD-LGBTQ-friendly counselor or psychotherapist?

Eva: First of all, look for a therapist who specializes in ASD-LGBTQ or at least ASD in adults. The majority of clinicians work with children on the spectrum and have very little experience with adults who do not have immediately obvious autistic behaviors. Many times, my clients will tell me that their former therapist, couple's counselor or psychiatrist ruled out that they might be on the spectrum because they made eye-contact, had friends, had a relationship and/or had a successful career. Or a couple's counselor might say to the spouse, "I see that your partner has empathy because she just offered you a tissue when you started to tear up. I don't think they're autistic!" So, it's really important to find someone who really gets the experiences of autistic adults, their family members, and partners.

Second, find someone who's willing to listen and learn, even if they aren't a specialist. An open, empathetic, and accepting therapist can sometimes make all the difference. Also, a good therapist will admit that they may not have all the answers if they're not an expert in a particular area. They may refer you to additional resources, as well as encourage and facilitate your search for the information you need. And lastly, it's quite alright to find another therapist if the one you go to isn't affirming or doubts your identities.

Appendix

Mendes and Maroney Autism Spectrum Difference (ASD) Diagnostic Key

The following diagnostic key can be used by clinicians and mental health to form an ASD diagnosis. Those seeking to understand themselves better within the framework of ASD may use this key to self-diagnose as well. Please note that ASD traits vary in severity and quantity and manifest uniquely in each individual. It's better to view ASD as a cluster of traits rather than a linear spectrum where a person meets all traits. It's important to view the traits in the larger context of the individual's family of origin and life experiences, and find out how the traits pose challenges in the areas of work, academics, life skills, and relationships. We therefore recommend that a diagnosis is best conducted by someone who specializes in ASD, given the complexity with which the individual's life and traits intersect.

Core Features of ASD in the Following Areas:	
	Behavioral Manifestation of the Spectrum of Traits
1. Social	☐ Need a lot of alone time ☐ May struggle making friends or maintaining friendships, or make one or two friends through work/special interests ☐ Struggle with social reciprocity ☐ Prefer to work/play alone vs. with peers ☐ May put on gregarious/scripted persona when at a social event ☐ May need alcohol/drugs to relax/socially interact at a party ☐ May experience confusion/trouble adjusting behavior to suit social context ☐ May have problems inferring or misunderstanding the intentions of others* ☐ Face challenges navigating social situations, especially new and unexpected, or need to prepare ahead of time ☐ Lose interest in other people's experiences and narrative* ☐ Prefer to use technology to interact with others ☐ Favor one-to-one conversations vs. group ☐ Confused by, oblivious to, or disagree with societal norms ☐ Susceptible to conflicts with others
2. Communication	☐ May overtalk, monopolize, not realize that others are uninterested ☐ Struggle to understand intent and context of what is said to them ☐ Interrupt conversations to correct details, or facts ☐ Take what is said literally, often losing context ☐ Do not like small talk or casual conversation ☐ Struggle to initiate conversations ☐ Difficulty with back and forth conversation flow ☐ Use communication to inform rather than connect ☐ Trouble expressing thoughts and feelings spontaneously ☐ May often miss the main point of the discussion ☐ Struggle to get the emotions/subtleties in conversations ☐ Trouble hearing/understanding tone of voice ☐ Highly logical and erudite ☐ No filter; can inadvertently make insensitive comments ☐ Can get loud without meaning to when excited or upset ☐ May speak in a monotone ☐ Short attention span around topics that are not focused on their special interests or work ☐ Miss nonverbal cues ☐ Confused by people's facial expressions or body language

3. Emotional Regulation	☐ Trouble regulating emotions
	☐ Emotions escalate from zero to 60!
	☐ May display selective mutism when stressed, or after a meltdown
	☐ Extremely placid or even-tempered; no emotional expression whatsoever
	☐ Poor emotional reciprocity
	☐ Anger/rage issues
	☐ Lack emotional, cognitive and psychological self-awareness*
	☐ May have difficulty putting emotions into words
	☐ Poor awareness of own emotions
	☐ Can come off as cold and unfeeling
	☐ Vulnerable to stress
	☐ Prone to meltdowns due to certain stress/anxiety/cognitive triggers
	☐ Unaware of others' feelings*
	☐ May struggle communicating/conveying empathy*
	☐ Susceptible to picking up other people's emotional state
	☐ Thin-skinned and highly sensitive
	☐ Predisposed to depression
	☐ Almost always anxious
4. Cognitive; includes Theory of Mind and Central Coherence	☐ Trouble explaining one's own behaviors*
	☐ Difficulty predicting the behavior or emotional state of others*
	☐ Difficulty understanding/taking the perspectives of others*
	☐ Not understanding how behavior impacts others' thinking/feeling*
	☐ Struggle with joint attention
	☐ Preference for and excel at focusing on extreme details**
	☐ Adept at picking out a tiny element from complicated data sets**
	☐ Trouble getting the global meaning from details**
	☐ Delayed developmental milestones in childhood and as an adult
	☐ May have trouble launching into adult life
	☐ Have a childlike quality; may be naive and gullible
	☐ Given to cognitive distortions
	☐ Linear thinking patterns
	☐ Seek precision in speech
	☐ Black and white (all or nothing) thinking
	☐ Rigid/inflexible thinking and point of view
	☐ Tendency to perseverate on details or negatives of a person or situation
	☐ Slow processing around communication, especially if of a social or emotional nature
	☐ Have an "elephant's memory" for details
	☐ Can be obsessed with social justice issues, news, and finances
	☐ Unaware of/confused by cause and effect
	☐ Mild paranoia; assuming the worst
	☐ May have an "intuitive knowing" and may be highly sensitive to negative vibes/intent
	☐ Atypical ways of coping; addictions to video games, sex, porn, special interests

Core Features of ASD in the Following Areas:	Behavioral Manifestation of the Spectrum of Traits
5. Structure, Routine, Repetition, and Rigidity	☐ Attachment to routines, objects, or structure ☐ Hard time switching schedules ☐ Need structure ☐ Insistence on sameness, for example, sitting in the same spot ☐ Need to know when exactly things start and end ☐ Fixated on the same idea, even when proven otherwise ☐ Tend to perseverate on the past (have trouble letting go of thoughts) ☐ Ruminate/magnify negative facts ☐ Intense, fixed special interest in a particular subject or categories (e.g. cars, exercise, money, video games, etc; interests could change over time) ☐ Trouble switching attention, compromising, and negotiating ☐ Ritualized, OCD-like behaviors ☐ Resistant to trying new things ☐ Echolalia, i.e. repeating odd phrases or sentences they may have heard somewhere to self-soothe or because they like the sound
6. Executive Functioning	☐ Difficulty with task initiation ☐ Struggle with pacing self, too slow or too fast ☐ Trouble managing time ☐ Trouble managing space ☐ Difficulty with planning and prioritization ☐ Extremely messy ☐ Highly fastidious ☐ Hoarder ☐ Minimalist ☐ Always punctual ☐ Arrive way ahead of time ☐ Chronically late ☐ Too much awareness of time ☐ Too little awareness of time ☐ May feel like they're floating through time ☐ Misplace important objects ☐ Trouble managing financial basics ☐ Have trouble figuring out how long a task would take ☐ Struggle mapping out steps for a task ☐ Absent-minded and forgetful about tasks of daily living ☐ Hard to shift focus from one task to another ☐ Trouble with working memory (recalling things at the right moment) ☐ Struggle to multitask and can only focus on one thing at a time

7. Sensory	☐ Hyper- or hypo-sensitivity to touch, sound, sight, smell, taste ☐ May not like light touch ☐ May be overly ticklish ☐ May enjoy and need sensory input like deep pressure or hugs, and weighted blankets ☐ Have trouble with certain fabrics and tags on clothing ☐ May struggle with sensory sensitivities to clothes ☐ May wear a "uniform"; have no interest in clothes ☐ May be well dressed and interested in fashion ☐ Notice sounds that others do not ☐ May be triggered by loud noises to the point of a meltdown ☐ Extremely sensitive to certain smells ☐ Sensitive to light ☐ Poor or superior visuo-spatial ability ☐ Taste and texture can be hard to palate ☐ Fussy with food and may eat the same thing over and over again
8. Physical	☐ Awkward gait, body language, and expression ☐ Unintentional or subconscious repetitive motor movements ☐ Rigid/clumsy movements ☐ Lack body intelligence ☐ Inconsistent/atypical eye-contact (staring or not making enough eye-contact) ☐ Habitual rocking, flapping, tapping, picking behaviour in order to self-regulate ☐ Odd hand gestures ☐ May not like to be touched or hugged ☐ Love sex ☐ Dislike sex ☐ Asexual ☐ Gray sexual; low sex drive ☐ Require a lot of physical exercise ☐ Extremely sedentary ☐ Needing sensory input like deep pressure in the forms of deep hugs, massage, intense yoga, weight-lifting, or exercise ☐ May have gastrointestinal issues

Core Features of ASD in the Following Areas:	Behavioral Manifestation of the Spectrum of Traits
9. Academic	☐ Students with ASD tend to have good rote memory ☐ Struggle to learn abstract language and concepts such as idioms and sarcasm ☐ Reading comprehension challenges ☐ Writing open-ended topics can be challenging ☐ Struggle to brainstorm new ideas and problem-solve independently, especially if not their special interest ☐ Students with ASD may be easily distracted ☐ Don't pay attention to the right information ☐ Hyper-focused on certain details vs. the big picture ☐ Trouble shifting attention from one task to another ☐ Difficulty with transitions ☐ Struggle to conclude preferred activities ☐ Struggle to adapt to new skills ☐ Severe cognitive deficits ☐ Giftedness and high IQ ☐ Learn in a sequence different from peers ☐ Students with ASD often struggle to generalize between situations and people ☐ Must be explicitly taught skills within each environment ☐ Learn best through repetition ☐ Visual learners and processors; prefer step-by-step, illustrated instructions
10. Work	☐ Workaholic or over-focused on work, often out of habit, but also if work is a special interest ☐ Do not know when to stop; can work 24/7 if not checked ☐ Can work themselves to exhaustion ☐ Trouble rationing energy ☐ Prioritize work over personal life ☐ Underemployed ☐ Trouble advocating at work ☐ Take instructions literally and try to "do it all" ☐ Susceptible to burnout ☐ May go through several careers/jobs ☐ Gravitate towards computers, science, engineering, medicine, design, inventing, technology, writing, art, music

<table>
<tr><td>11. Romantic Relationships</td><td>☐ May not want a relationship at all
☐ Do not know how to repair the relationship after a conflict
☐ May miss cues about how their partner is feeling
☐ Lack of social-emotional reciprocity
☐ Lack of romantic spontaneity
☐ Lack of spontaneous sharing
☐ May not initiate spending time with partner
☐ Trouble understanding and nurturing emotional side of the relationship
☐ Want a lot of sex
☐ Do not need any sex
☐ Frequent meltdowns
☐ May lack awareness of how their behavior affects the relationship
☐ Have trouble managing anxiety, depression, anger, OCD, and ADHD behaviors that negatively impact the relationship
☐ Poor self-awareness can mean that they may not speak up for their needs in the relationship, thereby overextending themselves
☐ Struggle to meet the emotional needs of the partner
☐ Trouble coping with sensory overload, often resulting in meltdowns that traumatize their partner
☐ Get sucked into spending time involved in special interests vs. their partner
☐ Need training and support to be in a relationship
☐ Need coaching/perspective to be a parent</td></tr>
<tr><td colspan="2">Traits and features may sometimes be fully or mildly manifested in childhood; traits may not be fully apparent until later in life when social requirements overtax the limited abilities of the individual (DSM-5, 2013). Traits might also be concealed by superficial coping mechanisms.</td></tr>
<tr><td colspan="2">Traits and features may cause notable and often severe challenges in social, academic, occupational, or/and interpersonal relationships (DSM-5, American Psychiatric Association, 2013). For those who are considered to be more high-functioning, traits may often only manifest most visibly in romantic relationships.</td></tr>
<tr><td colspan="2">Traits can interact with each other in order to create circumstances that can get very challenging to cope with. Often professional help is needed in the form of ASD literature, counseling, medications, and ASD-specific life-coaching in order to problem solve, apply strategies, and access resources.</td></tr>
</table>

*Theory of Mind traits

**Traits related to the theory of "Central Coherence"

Some traits and features were adapted from and influenced by the following resources: American Psychiatric Association (2013); Interactive Autism Network (n.d.); Mendes (2015); Mendes and Maroney (in press); Myhill and Jekel (n.d.); National Institute for Health Research (2012); Project Peak (2009); Simone (n.d)

References

American Psychiatric Association (2000) *Diagnostic and Statistical Manual of Mental Disorders: DSM-IV-TR*. Washington, DC: American Psychiatric Association.

American Psychiatric Association (2013) *Diagnostic and Statistical Manual of Mental Disorders* (*DSM-5*). Arlington, VA: American Psychiatric Publishing.

Armstrong, T. (2010) *Neurodiversity: Discovering the Extraordinary Gifts of Autism, ADHD, Dyslexia, and Other Brain Differences.* Philadelphia, PA: Da Capo Press.

AVEN (The Asexual Visibility and Education Network) (2018) Overview. Retrieved from https://www.asexuality.org/?q=overview.html on November 5, 2018.

Baio, J., Wiggins, L., Christensen, D. L., Maenner, M. J. *et al.* (2018) "Prevalence of autism spectrum disorder among children aged 8 years—Autism and developmental disabilities monitoring network, 11 Sites, United States, 2014." *MMWR Surveillance Summaries 67*, 6, 1.

Barnett, J. P. and Maticka-Tyndale, E. (2015) "Qualitative exploration of sexual experiences among adults on the autism spectrum: Implications for sex education." *Perspectives on Sexual and Reproductive Health 47*, 4, 171–179.

Bradford, J., Reisner, S. L., Honnold, J. A. and Xavier, J. (2013) "Experiences of transgender-related discrimination and implications for health: Results from the Virginia Transgender Health Initiative Study." *American Journal of Public Health, 103,* 10, 1820–1829.

Braun, V. and Clarke, V. (2006) "Using thematic analysis in psychology." *Qualitative Research in Psychology 3*, 2, 77–101.

Brody, J, (2016) Asking the right questions and decoding the answers: A strengths-based approach to gender identity when it overlaps with autism and other neurological variations. Workshop conducted in May at the Asperger/Autism Network, Watertown, MA.

Bumiller, K. (2008) "Quirky citizens: Autism, gender, and reimagining disability." *Signs: Journal of Women in Culture and Society 33*, 4, 967–991.

Budge, S. L. (2015) "Psychotherapists as gatekeepers: An evidence-based case study highlighting the role and process of letter writing for transgender clients." *Psychotherapy 52*, 3, 287–297.

Bush, H. H. (2016) "Self-reported sexuality among women with and without autism spectrum disorder (ASD)." Doctoral dissertation, University of Massachusetts Boston.

Clark, B. A., Veale, J. F., Greyson, D. and Saewyc, E. (2017) "Primary care access and foregone care: A survey of transgender adolescents and young adults." *Family Practice 35*, 3, 1–5.

D'amico, E., Julien, D., Tremblay, N. and Chartrand, E. (2015) "Gay, lesbian, and bisexual youths coming out to their parents: Parental reactions and youths' outcomes." *Journal of GLBT Family Studies 11*, 5, 411–437.

D'Augelli, A. R. (2002) "Mental health problems among lesbian, gay, and bisexual youths ages 14 to 21." *Clinical Child Psychology and Psychiatry 7*, 3, 433–456.

de Vries, A. L., Noens, I. L., Cohen-Kettenis, P. T., van Berckelaer-Onnes, I. A. and Doreleijers, T. A. (2010) "Autism spectrum disorders in gender dysphoric children and adolescents." *Journal of Autism and Developmental Disorders 40*, 8, 930–936.

DeWinter, J., De Graaf, H. and Begeer, S. (2017) "Sexual orientation, gender identity, and romantic relationships in adolescents and adults with autism spectrum disorder." *Journal of Autism and Developmental Disorders 47*, 9, 2927–2934.

DeWinter, J., Vermeiren, R., Vanwesenbeeck, I., Lobbestael, J. and Nieuwenhuizen, C. (2015) "Sexuality in adolescent boys with autism spectrum disorder: Self-reported behaviours and attitudes." *Journal of Autism and Developmental Disorders 45*, 3, 731–741.

Gates, G. J. (2017) "In U.S., more adults identifying as LGBT." *Social and Policy Issues*, January 11. Retrieved from http://news.gallup.com/poll/201731/lgbt-identification-rises.aspx on June 30, 2018.

George, R., and Stokes, M. (2016). "'Gender Is Not on My Agenda!': Gender Dysphoria and Autism Spectrum Disorder." In L. Mazzoni and B. Vitiello (eds) *Psychiatric Symptoms and Comorbidities in Autism Spectrum Disorder.* New York: Springer.

George, R. and Stokes, M. A. (2017) "Gender identity and sexual orientation in autism spectrum disorder." *Autism 22*, 8, 970–982.

George, R. and Stokes, M. A. (2018) "Sexual orientation in autism spectrum disorder." *Autism Research 11*, 1, 133–141.

Giles, D. C. (2014) "'DSM-V is taking away our identity': The reaction of the online community to the proposed changes in the diagnosis of Asperger's disorder." *Health 18*, 2, 179–195.

Gillespie-Lynch, K., Kapp, S. K., Brooks, P. J., Pickens, J. and Schwartzman, B. (2017) "Whose expertise is it? Evidence for autistic adults as critical autism experts." *Frontiers in Psychology* 8, 1–14.

Gilmour, V., Schalomon, P. M. and Smith, V. (2011) "Sexuality in a community based sample of adults with autism spectrum disorder." *Research in Autism Spectrum Disorders 6*, 1, 313–318.

GLAAD (2016) GLAAD media reference guide. Retrieved from www.glaad.org/sites/default/files/GLAAD-Media-Reference-Guide-Tenth-Edition.pdf on November 5, 2018.

Gougeon, N. A. (2010) "Sexuality and autism: A critical review of selected literature using a social-relational model of disability." *American Journal of Sexuality Education 5*, 4, 328–361.

Hellemans, H., Colson, K., Verbraeken, C., Vermeiren, R. and Deboutte, D. (2007) "Sexual behavior in high-functioning male adolescents and young adults with autism spectrum disorder." *Journal of Autism and Developmental Disorders 37*, 2, 260–269.

Hillier, A., Gallop, N., Mendes, E., Buckingham, A., Nizami, A. and O'Toole, D. (2018) "LGBTQI and Autism Spectrum Disorder: Experiences and Challenges." Manuscript submitted for publication, University of Massachusetts Lowell, Department of Psychology.

Human Rights Watch (2018) *LGBT rights.* Retrieved from www.hrw.org/topic/lgbt-rights on July 1, 2018.

Interactive Autism Network (IAN) (n.d.) "Cognitive Theories Explaining ASD." Retrieved from https://iancommunity.org/cs/understanding_research/cognitive_theories_explaining_asds on May 2, 2018.

Janssen, J., Huang, H. and Duncan, C. (2016) "Gender variance among youth with autism spectrum disorders: A retrospective chart review." *Transgender Health 1*, 1, 63–68.

Jefferson, K., Neilands, T. B. and Sevelius, J. (2013) "Transgender women of color: Discrimination and depression symptoms." *Ethnicity and Inequalities in Health and Social Care 6*, 4, 121–136.

Jennings, J. (2017) *Being Jazz: My Life as a (Transgender) Teen.* New York: Ember.

Jones, L., Goddard, L., Hill, E. L., Henry, L. A. and Crane, L. (2014) "Experiences of receiving a diagnosis of autism spectrum disorder: A survey of adults in the United Kingdom." *Journal of Autism and Developmental Disorders 44*, 12, 3033–3044.

Jones, R. M., Wheelwright, S., Farrell, K., Martin, E. *et al.* (2012) "Brief report: Female-to-male transsexual people and autistic traits." *Journal of Autism and Developmental Disorders 42*, 2, 301–306.

Katz-Wise, S. L., Ehrensaft, D., Vetters, R., Forcier, M. and Austin, S. B. (2018) "Family functioning and mental health of transgender and gender-nonconforming youth in the trans teen and family narratives project." *The Journal of Sex Research 5*, 4–5, 1–9.

Klein, A. and Golub, S. A. (2016) "Family rejection as a predictor of suicide attempts and substance misuse among transgender and gender nonconforming adults." *LGBT Health 3*, 3, 193–199.

Kuvalanka, K. A., Mahan, D. J., McGuire, J. K. and Hoffman, T. K. (2017) "Perspectives of mothers of transgender and gender-nonconforming children with autism spectrum disorder." *Journal of Homosexuality 65*, 9, 1–23.

Kreiser, N. L. and White, S. W. (2014) "ASD in females: Are we overstating the gender difference in diagnosis?" *Clinical Child and Family Psychology Review 17*, 1, 67–84.

Lehnhardt, F. G., Gawronski, A., Pfeiffer, K., Kockler, H., Schilbach, L. and Vogeley, K. (2013) "The investigation and differential diagnosis of Asperger syndrome in adults." *Deutsches Arzteblatt International 110*, 45, 755–763.

Mandell, D. S., Wiggins, L. D., Carpenter, L. A., Daniels, J. *et al.* (2009) "Racial/ethnic disparities in the identification of children with autism spectrum disorders." *American Journal of Public Health 99*, 3, 493–498.

Maroney, M. R. and Horne, S. G. (2018) Gender is a "Weird Social Thing That Didn't Jive with Me Being Autistic: The Identity Development and Experiences of Transgender and Autistic Adults." Manuscript in preparation.

Mendes, E. (2015) *Marriage and Lasting Relationships with Asperger's Syndrome (Autism Spectrum Disorder).* London: Jessica Kingsley Publishers.

Mendes, E. and Bush, H. H. (2016) "'Labels do not describe me': Gender identity and sexual orientation among women with Asperger's and autism." Retrieved from www.evmendes.com/publication on October 7, 2017.

Mendes, E. A. and Maroney, M. R. (in press) "At the Intersection of the Autism Spectrum and Sexual and Gender Diversity: Case Studies for Use with Clinicians and Clients." In J. Whitman and C. Boyd (eds) *The Therapist's Notebook for Sexual and Gender Identity Diverse Clients.* New York: Harrington Park Press.

Miller, H. R. (2015) "How to be an LGBT Ally." Retrieved from www.hrc.org/blog/how-to-be-an-lgbt-ally on March 5, 2018.

Myhill, G. and Jekel, D. (n.d.) "Neurology Matters: Recognizing, understanding, and treating neurodiverse couples in therapy." Retrieved from https://docs.wixstatic.com/ugd/6d3c85_d92f92a74dd64c49895434bdf7733e22.pdf on May 2, 2018.

National Institute for Health Research (2012) "AQ-10 Autism Spectrum Quotient (AQ)." Retrieved from http://docs.autismresearchcentre.com/tests/AQ10.pdf on May 2, 2018.

Ortega, F. (2009) "The cerebral subject and the challenge of neurodiversity." *BioSocieties 4*, 4, 425–445.

Parsloe, S. M. (2015) "Discourses of disability, narratives of community: Reclaiming an autistic identity online." *Journal of Applied Communication Research 43*, 3, 336–356.

Project Peak. (2009) "Learning characteristics of students with autism spectrum disorders." Retrieved from www.deercreekschools.org/UserFiles/Servers/Server_37435/File/deer creek district/autism files/(2)Learning Characteristics Presentation.pdf on July 6, 2018.

Rood, B. A., Maroney, M. R., Puckett, J. A., Berman, A. K., Reisner, S. L. and Pantalone, D. W. (2017) "Identity concealment in transgender adults: A qualitative assessment of minority stress and gender affirmation." *American Journal of Orthopsychiatry 87*, 6, 704.

Rotello, G. and Gillis, J. R. (1997) "Sexual ecology: AIDS and the destiny of gay men." *The Canadian Journal of Human Sexuality 6*, 4, 335.

Rudolph, C. E., Lundin, A., Åhs, J. W., Dalman, C. and Kosidou, K. (2017) "Brief report: Sexual orientation in individuals with autistic traits: Population based study of 47,000 adults in Stockholm county." *Journal of Autism and Developmental Disorders 48*, 2, 619–624.

Ryan, C. (2009) "Helping families support their lesbian, gay, bisexual, and transgender (LGBT) children." *LGBT Brief*, Georgetown University. Retrieved from https://nccc.georgetown.edu/documents/LGBT_Brief.pdf on August 2, 2018.

Ryan, C., Huebner, D., Diaz, R. M. and Sanchez, J. (2009) "Family rejection as a predictor of negative health outcomes in white and Latino lesbian, gay, and bisexual young adults." *Pediatrics 123*, 1, 346–352.

Safe Zone Project (2018) Safe Zone training facilitator guide 5.0. Retrieved from https://thesafezoneproject.com/download-curriculum on August 2, 2018.

Shilo, G. and Savaya, R. (2011) "Effects of family and friend support on LGB youths' mental health and sexual orientation milestones." *Family Relations 60*, 3, 318–330.

Silberman, S. (2015) *Neurotribes: The Legacy of Autism and the Future of Neurodiversity.* New York: Avery, an imprint of Penguin Random House.

Simone, R. (n.d.) List of Female Asperger Syndrome Traits. Retrieved from http://help4aspergers.com/female-as-traits on September 2, 2015.

Strang, J. F., Kenworthy, L., Daniolos, P., Case, L. *et al.* (2012) "Depression and anxiety symptoms in children and adolescents with autism spectrum disorders without intellectual disability." *Research in Autism Spectrum Disorders 6*, 1, 406–412.

Strang, J. F., Meagher, H., Kenworthy, L., de Vries, A. L. *et al.* (2016) "Initial clinical guidelines for co-occurring autism spectrum disorder and gender dysphoria or incongruence in adolescents." *Journal of Clinical Child and Adolescent Psychology 47*, 1, 105–115.

Steinmetz, K. (2017) "Why transgender people are being murdered at a historic rate." *Time*, August 17. Retrieved from http://time.com/3999348/transgender-murders-2015, on July 1, 2018.

Turban, J. L. and van Schalkwyk, G. I. (2018) "'Gender dysphoria' and autism spectrum disorder: Is the link real?" *Journal of the American Academy of Child and Adolescent Psychiatry 57*, 1, 8–9.

Urquhart, E. (2016) "Gatekeepers vs. informed consent: Who decides when a trans person can medically transition?" Retrieved from www.slate.com/blogs/outward/2016/03/11/transgender_patients_and_informed_consent_who_decides_when_transition_treatment.html on March 6, 2018.

Veaux, F., Rickert, E. and Hardy, J. W. (2014) *More Than Two: A Practical Guide to Ethical Polyamory.* Portland, OR: Thorntree Press, LLC.

Virupaksha, H. G., Muralidhar, D. and Ramakrishna, J. (2016) "Suicide and suicidal behavior among transgender persons." *Indian Journal of Psychological Medicine 38*, 6, 505–509.

Willey, L. H. (2012) *Safety Skills for Asperger Women: How to Save a Perfectly Good Female Life.* London: Jessica Kingsley Publishers.

Zakalik, R. A. and Wei, M. (2006) "Adult attachment, perceived discrimination based on sexual orientation, and depression in gay males: Examining the mediation and moderation effects." *Journal of Counseling Psychology 53*, 3, 302.

Subject Index

Author Index